MANAGEMENT

BRIAN PINDER-AYRES

IBA Publishing

Financial Management

© RIBA Enterprises Ltd 2016

Published by RIBA Publishing, part of RIBA Enterprises Ltd, The Old Post Office, St Nicholas Street, Newcastle upon Tyne, NE1 1RH

ISBN 978 1 85946 602 5

Stock code 84985

The right of Brian Pinder-Ayres to be identified as the Author of this Work has been asserted in accordance with the Copyright, Designs and Patents Act 1988 sections 77 and 78.

All rights reserved. No part of this publication may be reproduced, stored in a retrieval system, or transmitted, in any form or by any means, electronic, mechanical, photocopying, recording or otherwise, without prior permission of the copyright owner.

British Library Cataloguing-in-Publication Data
A catalogue record for this book is available from the British Library.

Publisher: Steven Cross
Commissioning Editor: Sharla Plant
Production: Richard Blackburn
Designed & typeset by Kalina Norton/Studio Kalinka
Illustrations by Peter Harpley
Printed and bound by CPI Antony Rowe in Chippenham, Great Britain

While every effort has been made to check the accuracy and quality of the information given in this publication, neither the Author nor the Publisher accept any responsibility for the subsequent use of this information, for any errors or omissions that it may contain, or for any misunderstandings arising from it.

www.ribaenterprises.com

CONTENTS

FINANCIAL
MANAGEMENT

FOREWORD

Running an architecture business effectively is not just a matter of pursuing 'profit' or 'staying afloat'- there is an ethical issue at stake too. Honouring your promises to staff, consultants and other suppliers and paying them on time is a mark of your integrity. Expecting your clients to pay you promptly while your staff have to wait for their money, or work long hours for nothing, is evidence of double standards.

In this lucid and practical book about a difficult subject, Brian Pinder-Ayres draws on his diverse experience of medium-sized practices and the tax affairs of many smaller firms, and offers a range of proven, effective tools for keeping track of cash, looking ahead and minimising risk.

He says: 'All of the architects I have ever met have been far more concerned about the quality of the finished building and its design integrity than about the making of money' (page 8). His observation that 'The vast majority of businesses that go under simply run out of cash' (page 9), leads inevitably to the maxim: 'Cashflow is the lifeblood of the practice' (page 60). If you need to remember one thing about this subject, it's probably that.

Financial management of architectural practice is not simple. It is complex, and we underestimate it at our peril. It should be imaginative and creative, but rigorous - just like architecture.

Steven Pidwill,
Shepheard Epstein Hunter

SERIES EDITORS' FOREWORD

By virtue of you picking up this book on Financial Management, you are either curious about the prospect of setting up in practice or are in practice, but want to have a better understanding of the numbers and a cost effective oracle on your shelf. Dealing with the finances along with business development are perhaps the two areas of start-up that Architects fear the most. This is most likely because many of us have not been taught this in our architectural education.

Financial Management has been written with a view to making this crucial aspect of running and sustaining your business as integral to your creative practice as is design.

Architects tend to be nervous of fully embracing the discipline of financial management in case it somehow or other detracts from what they see as the main thrust of their practice.

However, far from turning you into an accountant, good financial management frees you up to be the creative practitioner that you aspire to be, whilst honing your entrepreneurial eye.
This book will equip you with the knowledge and confidence to free you from worrying how to pay your bills so that you can focus your energies on what you do best and then use the results of that productive time to attract more work thus ensuring financial stability - a virtuous circle!

Written in clear language Financial Management is an essential user guide that covers all the stages in the typical life cycle of a practice, from deciding which form of business to adopt through annual budgeting and fee setting to succession planning. Within its pages are the tools to deal with the concepts, language and a good steer on how to manage both your accounts and accountant relationships. The humorous illustrations throughout are complemented by worked examples and definitions thereby making the detailed information accessible without resort to financial jargon.

Del Hossain and Anne Markey

ABOUT THE SERIES EDITORS

Anne Markey is a director of Phelan Architects, a practice she founded in 2009 with her husband Brendan Phelan. She also heads up the Projects Office within the Sir John Cass Faculty of Art, Architecture and Design at London Metropolitan University, and has over twenty years experience as an architect. Anne is a member of the RIBA and sits on the RIBA CPD Sub-Committee. She is a board member of Catalyst Housing, one of the leading housing associations within London and the South East, where her role is that of Design Champion.

Del Hossain is the MD of the Adrem Group a leading International Architecture and Design Careers Agency based in London, Dubai and Shanghai. By background he is an Architect having practiced with some of London's leading design firms including Foster and Partners and ORMS. In 2012 he was Awarded 'London's Business Mentor of the Year' for developing companies with a social agenda and progressive ambitions. Del is also a qualified Organisational Development and Wellbeing Psychologist and works closely with leadership teams and Directors in the Creative Industries on their People Strategies and team motivation. He is also a speaker at numerous universities and a former Chairman of the Bartlett Alumni. Del is the Joint Editor of the RIBA's Business Books Series.

ABOUT THE AUTHOR

Brian Pinder-Ayres qualified as a chartered management accountant (ACMA) in 1984 while working as a finance and tax analyst with Mobil North Sea Ltd. He has held the most senior management roles in finance with Polaroid, Braxton Associates (the strategy consulting arm of major accountancy practice Deloitte) and a firm of niche-market City solicitors Walton & Morse LLP. For five years he worked as a management consultant with chartered accountants Moores Rowland during which time he specialised in advising professional firms on a wide variety of financial management issues.

Brian joined YRM Architects just after their successful management buyout in 1997, and established the finance function for the new business. In 2001, he took up the role of Finance Director at architects and planners Shepheard Epstein Hunter plc. He has lectured on finance and architectural practice to students studying for the RIBA Part 3 examination at Portsmouth University, Cambridge University and London South Bank University and is a regular contributor to the very successful annual Part 3 programme at the University of Westminster. He also lectures in financial management for the RIBA.

ACKNOWLEDGEMENTS

Over the years, one of my strongest and lasting impressions when working with architects is their openness and generosity. I have always appreciated their willingness to take the time to share their knowledge and experience of practice with me, often in the form of amusing or terrifying anecdotes.

I am particularly indebted to my fellow directors and colleagues at Shepheard Epstein Hunter and to the former directors of YRM Architects for their help, advice and support. I am well aware that much of what I have learnt - and which I am now putting forward in this book - originally came from them. I have also taken a lot from the feedback of the Part 3 students who have attended my lectures over the years. Their questions and comments have helped me to focus on the areas of practice that are obviously uppermost in their minds and identify the issues that seem to trouble them the most.

As ever I need to thank my wife Liz for her unfailing patience, encouragement and support throughout this project.

A HEALTHY TENSION

INTRODUCTION

THE SPECIAL CHALLENGES OF ARCHITECTURAL PRACTICE

It has always seemed to me that the practice of architecture demands a far wider and more diverse set of skills than is generally required by most other professions.

Successful lawyers will have developed sharp analytical skills that allow them to follow principle and precedent in the logical pursuit of the argument in the case. The law touches every aspect of our lives, but the application of legal skills is much the same no matter which area of the law an individual may choose to practise in. The successful accountant will obviously have a facility with figures and an ability to 'think with the numbers'. Hopefully this will be coupled with an ability to communicate the significance of the figures to colleagues in other disciplines. Again, the potential numbers of fields of application are many, but the core skills remain much the same.

By contrast, successful architects need the skills to be equally at home with blue sky conceptual design and the production of detailed drawings in which tolerances can be as small as a couple of millimetres. They need to be able to visualise a building or whole scheme that could affect the quality of the lives of thousands of people over many years to come. Furthermore, they need to be able to communicate this vision to their potential clients. This communication has to be sufficiently dynamic and exciting to persuade those clients to invest very large sums of money in their vision. They may well have performed this minor miracle initially with little more than an outline sketch drawn freehand on a blank piece of paper.

In addition, architects need to combine all these talents with an ability to perform repetitive tasks with great accuracy. For example, they may have to produce door schedules that fit in with the overall design, but which also fit in to the openings provided for them when they are delivered to the site. They need to have an understanding of the nature and quality of the materials they are specifying and an appreciation of the environmental impact and implications of the choices they are making. These are all quite distinct skills, yet the successful architect will be required to have a command of them all. This is especially true for architects in small practices where the limited number of staff means that functional specialisation is a luxury that cannot normally be afforded.

Architects also need to be able to get on with a wide range of people and situations. As design team leaders they have to reconcile many conflicting agendas and demands to achieve a balance that leads to a practical solution. The architect stands alone on the conductor's podium with baton in hand and attempts to bring the orchestra of clients, planners, contractors, engineers, surveyors and their own staff together to produce a coherent symphony. All this despite the fact that each of these groups appears to have different versions of the music in front of them and never all seem to be playing at the same time!

These conflicts must be constantly managed and this is reflected in the financial management practice too. As in any other business the aim is to steer towards the desired financial destination and to keep progress towards it as steady as possible.

However, there are many potential traps and surprises that lie in wait during the construction of a building to drive even the best laid plans off course at any time.

Apparently an aeroplane making a transatlantic flight is technically off course about 80 per cent of the time. It's the pilot's job to keep making constant corrections so that everyone arrives as intended in New York rather than in Miami. Financial managers too have to be constantly vigilant, and be prepared to make the necessary corrections along the financial journey. Their job is to develop a set of tools and indicators that will quickly show whether the practice is going off course, and where to look to find a solution to the problem.

As a finance professional, I live in an analytical world. The world of money is inextricably linked with the passage of time. Costs are measured and accumulated on a time-driven basis; staff and rent or mortgage commitments need to be met each month; utility bills must be paid quarterly and professional indemnity insurance and professional subscriptions are due annually. Every cost that is incurred has its own timetable and there are unpleasant consequences for not sticking to the schedule.

I prepare a five-year financial plan from which I derive the annual budget for our practice. From the budget I can extract monthly forecasts of income and expenditure and consequent cash flow. This may lead in turn to weekly plans showing which projects will be occupying the staff that week. In short: I am constantly aware of the relationship between time and money.

But this is where tension arises. As an architectural practice we expect and, for a while, we want our architect colleagues to 'lose track of time' and to get carried away with the excitement of the creative process. It is in this mode that they are the most likely to produce their best work.

Yet we are also acutely aware that our financial obligations accrue relentlessly on a daily basis and that it is our responsibility to ensure that we will have the funds available to meet them when they become due.

So I see a major part of my financial management role as the creation and management of a healthy tension. Without damaging or distracting from the creative process, I need to be constantly reminding the team that there are time and budget constraints that we all have to live with. Ultimately, we will have failed if we end up with the most magnificent design that we cannot realise because we have bankrupted the practice before we got the chance to bring it into being.

We need an atmosphere in which innovative design can flourish. But we also need it to be understood that there is usually simply not enough time or budget to go through that process two or three times before settling on a design solution. We also need to guard against a failure to complete the design process at the appropriate stage of the project. I have seen the dire consequences of designing 'on the hoof' at the working drawings stage. This is bound to result in change and confusion which will lead to delay and additional cost.

All architects will, at some point, need to grapple with financial spreadsheets and take tough business decisions, whether they work in large practices or are sole traders. This book aims to present an overview of basic business finance, as applicable to the architecture profession, and I set out the ground rules for establishing a practice on firm foundations and driving it forward into a prosperous future. Along the way, I address the thorny question of 'how much to charge clients', give pointers on credit control and even invite you to consider the ultimate future of the business and your role within it.

I hope that you find the book a useful resource and keep dipping in and out of its pages over the years. However, most of the examples are versions of the way I work in practice at Shepheard Epstein Hunter (SEH), and fit together in a logical progression, so I highly recommend that you first read it from beginning to end, so that you have a thorough grounding in the basics.

I wrote the original version of this book, then titled *Painless Financial Management*, in 2008 and it was published just before the world-wide recession changed the financial landscape for us all. Although we all know that the construction industry is cyclical and that there will be ups and downs, nothing could have prepared us for the way the world changed. Since then, the pace of change has escalated considerably, and there has been an increase in business uncertainty coupled with a growth in self-employment, flexible working and many start-up companies. There has rarely been a more urgent need for creative professionals to get a firm grip on their finances, and this book aims to set you on the right path – with the tools to help you adjust course whichever way the financial future turns.

THREE WAY CHOICE

01

SETTING UP

SETTING UP IN PRACTICE

The decision to set up an architectural practice is a major, and probably life-changing, decision and there are many factors to be considered. This chapter focuses on the financial consequences and significance of the choice of business form. The initial choice you make will have fundamental implications for the practice throughout its lifetime. It will ultimately be of great significance to you or the person who started the business when the time comes to leave or retire.

The chapter also begins to introduce you to the core financial decisions that every practice needs to take.

CHOOSING THE RIGHT FORM OF BUSINESS FOR YOU

There are three main business structures available to you when you decide to set up a practice:

› Sole trader or partnership

› Limited liability partnership (LLP)

› Limited company (Ltd).

SOLE TRADER AND PARTNERSHIP

The simplest business form of practice is as a sole trader or as a group of sole traders who form a simple partnership. Each of the individuals involved is self-employed and responsible for their own tax affairs.

All self-employed people have to register with HM Revenue & Customs (HMRC) for self-assessment, which means that they will then have to submit an annual tax return that declares their business profits along with any other taxable income. It is important to register with the tax office within three months of starting to 'trade', otherwise a £100 penalty could be applied – which would not be a great way to start your commercial relationship with HMRC.

www.gov.uk/hmrc

For an individual architect starting out on their own, being self-employed is usually the sensible way to begin, because you will have many other things to think about other than the complexities of trading via a limited company or limited liability partnership (LLP).

The great disadvantage of this business form, for architects, is the potentially unlimited personal liability that you're exposing yourself to. Although you will, of course, have professional indemnity insurance (PII) in place, there are a number of other scenarios under which you could find yourself being successfully sued for a significant amount of money. In these circumstances it would be possible to lose all of your personal assets including your home.

In the past, many architects operated quite happily for years as part of a simple partnership and managed to sleep at night, despite the 'joint and several' liability (where each person in a partnership is individually liable to pay back the entire amount of the partnership's debts or liabilities) which is a key ingredient of this particular form of practice. Sadly, the increasingly litigious world in which we now all live makes this an unacceptably risky model. It is widely known that professionals will have PII, and it is widely assumed that they and their insurers will also have deep pockets. This has made all professional advisers potentially attractive targets for financial claims. It was the solicitors and accountants who made up the profit-sharing ownership of the large multi-national firms that became especially concerned about this issue. They were the ones who led the campaign for the introduction of a new hybrid business model – LLP.

LIMITED LIABILITY PARTNERSHIP

In many ways, this business form is an attempt to give the professional practice the best of both worlds. Created by the Limited Liability Partnerships Act 2000, the LLP means that the partnership structure and ethos can be retained, with the addition of the all-important protection of limited liability for its members (partners), which is conveyed by its separate legal entity status. In simple terms, it means that the partners will not all risk losing their homes and other assets in the event of a successful claim against the practice which exceeds the level of their insurance cover.

As a consequence, the vast majority of the top 100 firms of solicitors and accountants have already converted to either LLP or limited company status. Traditionally, it was the fear of facing a very large professional indemnity claim that professional practitioners were most worried about. However, in a recent survey of legal firms that have been through the limited liability conversion process, the reason most commonly cited for conversion was the fear of the potentially unlimited damages that can result from an employment-related claim for unfair dismissal or discrimination.

Unsurprisingly then, this trend has also spread to the other people-based professions and a significant number of architects' practices have converted to LLPs over the past 15 years. If I were advising a group of architects who were contemplating establishing a new architectural practice today, I would strongly urge them to consider the potential benefits offered by an LLP.

The partners in an LLP continue to be treated for tax purposes as before (i.e. as self-employed individuals), and can carry on with the familiar regime of income tax paid via the self-assessment system. They have to submit a tax return by no later than 31 January following the end of the previous tax year on 5 April.

The LLP as an entity will also have to submit a tax return to reflect the overall profit situation of the business. This 'Partnership Tax Return' is used to identify how those profits or losses are shared between the individual partners, and the resulting figures then become the amounts to be entered in relation to partnership profits in each individual partner's self-assessment tax return.

In this way, partners in an LLP do not need to trouble themselves with the adjustment in thinking that is required by a limited company director, who has to become used to the different timings of the corporation tax regime and the delayed receipt of part of their remuneration in the form of dividends (often paid well after the end of the financial year).

One of the consequences of becoming an LLP is the requirement to file annual financial accounting information at Companies House. This will be the first step into the public domain for many and is sometimes cited as a reason to remain 'private' as a sole trader or partnership. Many professionals have been concerned that their peers and staff will be able to see how much (or perhaps even worse, how little) they have been earning. However, Companies House is well aware of these commercial sensitivities, and allows for highly abbreviated accounts information to be filed for all but the largest of companies or LLPs. For most small businesses, and therefore the vast majority of architects, this amounts to a basic Balance Sheet with a few technical notes. This is all that is available to be discovered by the public. In most cases it is very hard to deduce anything meaningful from these figures in terms of how well the practice is doing or how much an individual is earning.

www.gov.uk/companieshouse

As a part of the UK government's stated aim of reducing 'red tape' for small businesses these reporting thresholds are being revised upwards all the time. So the amount of information that is publicly available is set to be reduced even further in future years.

LIMITED COMPANY

The traditional alternative to working as a sole practitioner or in a partnership is to form a limited company.

As a practice grows in size and the amounts of money at stake become more substantial, a moment tends to be reached when it would make sense to everyone involved to seek the protection of limited personal liability which is provided by the setting up of a separate legal entity. This tends to be an organic process when a level of financial risk is reached at which everyone starts to feel uncomfortable.

The operation of a limited company does involve a degree of extra formality and the need to ensure compliance with the requirements of Companies House and HMRC. Company law has its origins in Victorian times and some of the language and procedures still seem quite antiquated. The Companies Act of 2006 attempted to modernise and simplify a lot of the systems. However, there will always be a price to be paid in terms of disclosure and public reporting, in return for the considerable benefits of limited liability.

Companies House has the task of keeping records on every company on its register so that any creditor or other interested party can find where the company is based, who owns it and the identity of its directors. In order to ensure that this information is kept up to date, Companies House has the power to fine companies for the late submission of information.
In extreme cases it has the power to take legal action against individual directors themselves.

Some architects may find it difficult to move from the familiar and informal cultural partnership to the more structured world of the limited company. Hence the appeal of the hybrid LLP described above.

In a limited company the ownership of the practice is reflected in the ownership of its shares. Shares can offer very useful flexibility, because circumstances change over the course of time. For instance, the more senior directors can sell or transfer their shares to the next generation of directors as part of a succession planning programme.

However, dealing with the changes in practice ownership via shares can be fraught with difficulty. Unless you have a shareholders' agreement in place that deals with all of the eventualities, very difficult issues can arise that revolve around the method used to place a value on the shares held. Very few architectural practices will be publicly listed on the stock exchange, so the value of an individual share becomes a very subjective judgement. The outgoing shareholder will, of course, wish to maximise the value they receive for the shares being sold. Equally, the acquiring shareholders will wish to buy the shares for the lowest possible price. Both parties will agree that a 'fair' price should be paid, but this is where the problems can begin, as each has quite different ideas of what a 'fair' method of calculation would be.

In order to avoid these problems it is wise to ensure that all new shareholders sign up to an agreement that specifies exactly how shares will change hands, and how the values to be used for this process will be calculated. Therefore it is well worth spending some money on good legal advice in this area, as disputes over shares and succession planning can paralyse the operation of a practice when management attention becomes internalised rather than staying focused on the needs of clients and the wider general market situation of the practice.

It is easy and inexpensive to set up a limited company online these days by following the simple process on the Companies House website. Indeed I often think that you could argue that it is frighteningly easy to do, given the legal and compliance obligations that follow as a result of this decision.

One pitfall to avoid when setting up the company is taking the option of setting up a company that is 'Limited by Guarantee'. I have known people who have done this, attracted by the idea of some sort of guarantee from Companies House which they assume makes this form of business safer. In fact this type of company is intended for not-for-profit businesses or organisations and is not generally suitable for architects in private practice. If a company Limited by Guarantee is set up it is not possible to transfer it into a company that is owned by shareholders. The initial company will need to be closed down and a new company set up in its place. This will be time consuming and could lead to problems with the use of names.

THE FUNDAMENTALS OF FINANCIAL MANAGEMENT

Having decided on the business model that best fits your current needs and future goals, it is essential that you understand the basics of financial management, including how to control 'working capital' and how to raise finance to invest in your business.

CONTROL OF WORKING CAPITAL

One of the key tasks in the financial management of a practice is the control of 'working capital'.

The total amount of money invested in the business is known as the capital. Some of this will be used to provide the permanent fixed assets that are required, such as buildings and vehicles, furniture or computer equipment. The balance goes to provide the funds to pay the staff and all the other day-to-day bills as they fall due. This is the everyday working money and in this book that is what I mean by 'working capital'.

DEFINITION: WORKING CAPITAL

Working capital is defined as the value of all *current assets* less the value of *current liabilities*.

The terms assets and liabilities are used in the preparation of the annual Balance Sheet, so it is possible to calculate working capital by looking at the most recently prepared set of financial accounts.

Current assets generally include:

- The cash balance at the bank
- The value of money owed to the practice by its customers (the debtors)
- The value of the work completed for which invoices have not yet been raised (often known as 'work in progress' but which is more correctly described as 'accrued income').

Current liabilities are the amounts owed to other people, which will mainly include:

- Staff (wages) or contractors (e.g. accountant, office cleaning company)
- Trade suppliers
- The tax authorities.

Liabilities will also include the amount paid to the bank under the terms of a short-term loan or overdraft. These people or organisations allow us some time to settle our obligations with them and thus to some extent are extending credit to us, hence the name 'creditors'.

In summary:

Working capital =

cash

+ debtors
(amounts owed to us by our customers)

+ accrued income
(work in progress)

– creditors
(amounts owed to suppliers).

In other words, working capital is the money you have in the bank plus the money that is owed by your customers and the value of the work completed but not yet invoiced, less the amount you owe to suppliers.

The key to the successful management of working capital is to find the correct balance between liquidity and profitability. For example, if you were to employ extra staff, you could undertake larger projects, which would hopefully result in greater profits. However, extra staff cost money and could prove to be very expensive if there are periods between projects when they cannot be usefully employed on fee-earning work.

How much working capital you need is determined by the overall level of fees. A good measure of how efficiently the practice is managing its financial resources is to calculate the working capital turnover rate. Simply divide the annual fee income by the average value of working capital over a year.

EXAMPLE: WORKING CAPITAL TURNOVER RATE

Total annual practice fee income = £200,000

Average working capital requirement during the year = £40,000

Working capital turnover rate = 5

In the above example the working capital circulated five times during the year, which could also be expressed as 'a 20 per cent turnover'.

This simple calculation means that you can now predict that if the practice were to increase its annual fees by a further £50,000, this would require a further 20 per cent in working capital (i.e. £10,000). This could be met in part from extra cash generated by the additional sales, but you may also require an increase in the practice's short-term borrowing or overdraft facility, which of course comes at a cost and begins to have a negative effect on profitability. Thus control of working capital is essential.

The level of working capital requirement can be managed in a different way. For instance, the amount of working capital required can be reduced by accelerating the rate at which money circulates through the business. In the example the money in the business turned over five times in the year, which equates to a working capital cycle of 73 days (365 days divided by 5). If you could speed up the cycle so that the money turned over 10 times (a 36-day cycle), that would also reduce the requirement for working capital to £20,000. In other words, the faster you collect the money owed by clients, the less working capital will be needed.

This is a crucial idea to understand, because it means that two otherwise identical practices could require quite different levels of working capital depending entirely on the efficiency with which they can manage the circulation of their funds. This will have a knock-on effect on their respective profitability because the less efficient practice will incur additional interest costs and thus make less money.

ACCELERATING THE WORKING CAPITAL CYCLE

By far the most effective way to speed up the working capital cycle (i.e. reduce the number of days) is to ensure that completed project work is billed promptly and regularly and that the resulting invoices are collected and converted into cash in the bank as rapidly as possible. The accounts function can assist to some degree by carefully taking advantage of all the credit that suppliers are prepared to give the practice. However, this is a limited process because there are costs involved in taking this too far. Taxes that are paid late will attract fines and interest charges and suppliers have a statutory right to punitive interest charges if their agreed payment terms are exceeded unless otherwise specifically agreed in the contract. We will look at the whole subject of credit control in more depth in Chapter 8.

MULTILEVEL MANAGEMENT

It is already evident that you need to be able to manage your architectural practice at a number of different levels simultaneously:

› You need to be able to track financial performance at project level, but also at a client or group level, as well as at the overall practice level.

› You also need to be able to add up the individual contributions from all the current projects to ensure that, in total, they will be sufficient to cover the overhead costs and generate enough profit to be reinvested in the growth and development of the practice.

There are now a number of software packages available (see Appendix: useful websites) to small and medium-sized practices that enable this to be done efficiently, and which also offer full integration with accounting and financial forecasting products. I am a strong advocate of these software products and believe that the time and money invested in buying and learning how to use them is easily justified and will translate into increased profitability for the practice very rapidly.

It is wise to devote some time and resources to gaining work through the competitive tendering process, because competition is fierce: only high-quality submissions are likely to win. It's also important to offer staff an opportunity to enter design competitions from time to time to enable them to develop their design skills at an early stage in their careers. Therefore, you need to ensure that you have allowed the time and budget to undertake projects which will not make much profit or indeed may cost money to undertake, if necessary.

So once again we find ourselves needing to manage conflicting demands and to deal with the financial consequences of this conflict. All of the architects I have ever met have been far more concerned about the quality of the finished building and its design integrity than about the making of money. So it is the overriding goal of financial management to ensure that the money flows smoothly and steadily through the practice, so that a lack of funds does not become a constraint on the growth and development of the practice.

One of my architect colleagues expressed it well by saying that 'good financial management creates the environment in which the architect can get on with the sort of design work that they want to do'. The alternative is to spend time worrying about how to pay the bills or to find yourself doing the sort of work you would rather not be involved with just because you need some money urgently to pay the staff or the rent.

RAISING FINANCE

One of the recurring themes in this book is that architectural practices tend to require more working capital than other businesses of a similar size, because of the extended time and payment periods that are involved in construction projects. As a consequence, architects will need more initial working capital and must constantly manage their cash flow very carefully if they are to keep out of trouble.

Experience shows that anyone starting a new business in whatever field tends to be wildly over-optimistic. We all underestimate how long it will take our customers to become as excited about what we have to offer as we are ourselves. We all tend to believe that our sales will build up more quickly than they actually do, and we also don't take into account how long it will take to get paid for the work that we have done.

Talking to bank relationship managers about how they approach start-up business plans can be very revealing. They are in the business of lending money to new businesses and they are fundamentally very keen to do so.

Most bank managers will have lending targets that they are keen to meet as their remuneration will depend in part on meeting those targets. However, they are well aware of the misplaced optimism on the part of their potential customers in relation to cash flow, especially in the early months and years.

In order to make adjustments for this 'exuberance factor' bank managers will look at the projected sales line on the forecast and discount it by one third or a half to see how this would affect cash flow. That gives the bank a much better indication of how much money the business is likely to need to borrow, and the manager can then apply the bank's own lending criteria to the adjusted set of figures to see if this is a business they still wish to finance.

Most start-up businesses will aim to finance their working capital requirements by means of an overdraft facility. This is often the most sensible option. The overdraft is intended to provide short-term fluctuating working capital finance. You may strongly regret any mismatch of finance arrangements when trading conditions become difficult and cash is tight.

Therefore, it is important to match the type of finance with the expenditure to which it relates. For example, it obviously makes sense to purchase property by using long-term finance such as a mortgage; it is also sensible to match the purchase of assets with a medium-term lifespan such as computers or furniture using a suitable three- or five-year term loan, rather than by further extending an overdraft.

The rapid development of online 'crowd funding' by websites such as RateSetter or Funding Circle opens a series of new funding opportunities for architects. A number of private and social housing projects have already been successfully financed in this way.

Studies of businesses of all types that have gone into insolvency reveal that only a few failed because they could not make a profit or had a poor business idea or model. The vast majority of businesses that go under simply run out of cash.

SUMMARY

› The choice of business form will have significant implications for the business from the outset. It will also affect the way that the owners can exit the practice when the time comes to leave or retire.

› Trading as a self-employed sole trader or partnership is simple and straightforward to understand but does come with unlimited personal liability. The limited liability company is the traditional solution to this problem, but this entails added complexity in the form of compliance with the requirements of Companies House and HMRC.

› The introduction of the limited liability partnership (LLP) offers a hybrid solution. Architectural practices can retain the look and feel of the partnership, while enjoying the protective cloak of limited personal liability.

› Management of the working capital cycle is crucial. Whatever you can do to speed up the rate at which money flows into and through the practice will reduce the total amount of money needed to finance the business.

- All businesses have to raise finance at the outset, and most tend to be over-optimistic about the level of sales they will achieve in the early years. Build this factor into the business plan and cash flow forecast that is used to approach the bank or other finance provider for overdraft facilities.
- Insufficient working capital from the outset could lead to problems in the early days of the practice.
- It is worth considering alternative forms of financing such as online crowd funding.
- New businesses tend to fail because they run out of cash.

02 FIRM FOUNDATIONS

THE FIRM FOUNDATIONS

The most important role for financial management in an architecture practice is the prediction of what lies ahead and an ability to communicate that prediction to the management of the practice so that they can respond accordingly. However, it is impossible to make meaningful forecasts if you don't have accurate historical information available as a starting point. The accounting process needs to show where you are now, and you need to have confidence in what you are being told, because you will construct a complex model of the future and make major decisions based on these foundations.

BASIC BOOK-KEEPING

Underpinning the whole financial process is the book-keeping system.

It does not matter if you are a sole practitioner or working in a practice with hundreds of staff, there has to be some reliable way of keeping the financial score. This is of course required by law in any event to satisfy our tax reporting obligations. The smallest of practices with only a few people involved may well be able to get by using simple spreadsheets to record lists of income and expenditure that can be translated into a final set of financial accounts at the end of the year by their accountant. Most practices of more than a few people will choose to use an accounting software package which performs the double-entry book-keeping in the background. These packages will also produce a preliminary Profit and Loss account and Balance Sheet. More sophisticated packages will combine accounting, time recording and project planning and reporting to provide an integrated approach to all of the financial aspects of the practice.

PROFIT AND LOSS ACCOUNT – A DEFINITION

This is the annual statement of income and expenditure that shows whether a practice has made an overall gain on its trading performance. It will show the profit or loss that has been made before tax, the tax charge (if any), and the subsequent profit after tax that is available for distribution to the owners or shareholders.

BALANCE SHEET – A DEFINITION

This is a statement of the total assets and liabilities of the business at a particular point in time (usually the end of the financial year). Assets are divided into *fixed assets* such as property and equipment and *current assets* which includes cash in the bank, amounts owed to the practice by its customers and the value of work in progress. The Balance Sheet balances by showing the net asset position and who owns those assets (usually the partners or shareholders of the practice).

A good book-keeping system will be:

- Simple to operate and maintain – entering information needs to be easy and the transition from one financial period or year to the next needs to be straightforward
- Detailed – containing enough information so that you can find items again later easily
- Logical – with items of a similar nature grouped together (e.g. the office expenses for gas, electricity and water will be next to each other in the accounts list rather than being spread out and mixed up with other types of expense)
- Up to date – credibility is soon lost if financial information is presented that can immediately be shown to be wrong because it is does not reflect the current situation
- Documented – each transaction should have a supporting original document (e.g. invoice or receipt).

Information must be recorded in a timely way, and there are a number of activities that need to happen on a routine basis. Gradually, this builds up over the course of the financial year so that you can produce the final output of the process – the annual accounts. The transactions and events that need to be recorded and a suggested timescale for each are listed opposite.

DAILY

- **Money received whether it is in the form of cheques or direct electronic payment**
- **Payment made either in the form of cash, cheque or bank transfer**
- **Invoices raised and sent to clients**
- **Invoices received from suppliers**

WEEKLY

- **Staff timesheets collected and entered**
- **Petty cash summarised**

MONTHLY

- **Payroll processing**
- **Staff expenses collected and reimbursed**
- **Bank reconciliation**

QUARTERLY

- **Value added tax (VAT) returns**

Reconciling your accounts with those of your bank - ensuring that all of the items on the statement have been recorded and that their records and yours agree - is crucial. One of the joys of modern accounting software is that this process can largely be automated. Bank statement data can be downloaded directly from the bank and the accounting software can gradually learn how to book transactions that occur regularly (e.g. the payment of rent).

MONTHLY PROFIT REPORTING

The gradual collection of all of this financial information is necessary so that you can produce a set of year-end accounts that will satisfy the requirements of all of the various stakeholders in the business.

However, this same information can also be used to provide management information that will allow you to make operating decisions during the course of the year.

There is a distinction to be drawn between the management accounting process and the financial accounting process. The latter aims to give a complete and 'true and fair view' of the business and is the most definitive statement of what happened financially during the year. This is produced mainly for compliance purposes and can often take a number of months to be finalised. By contrast, management information needs to be produced as soon after the period to which it relates as possible. Situations can change so rapidly within a practice that information relating to one month that is not available until three weeks after the end of that month (which used to be the norm) is almost of no value. Indeed, it could even be a hindrance because it could lead you to make decisions based on a set of circumstances that no longer apply.

So management information needs to be made available rapidly. I take the view that operating figures must be available within three working days of the end of the month.

There is usually a conscious trade-off between speed and detail. Even in the final published financial statements we do not have a truly accurate picture of events. We always have to make assumptions and exercise judgement about what values to include. Accountancy is an art rather than a science, and in the case of management accounts the chosen style is Impressionism rather than Realism.

You need to ensure that the major elements are reported as accurately as possible, but you do not need to be too concerned about glossing over some of the detail. In most practices the Pareto principle will apply (i.e. that roughly 80 per cent of the effects come from 20 per cent of the causes, as identified by the eponymous Italian philosopher in the 1890s). Expenditure on staff and premises will usually account for the majority of the regular monthly expenses and these amounts can be estimated with a fair degree of accuracy as soon as the month is complete.

Financial data only becomes useful information when it has been understood. It is important to consider the needs and preferences of your audience and to have an appreciation of how they assimilate information. The prime need is to communicate the big picture in as striking a way as possible and in my own practice we have developed a reporting format, shown below, that seems to work well. We call this a 'flash' report – in the sense of a newsflash, because it attempts to give the big picture in a rapid way.

Monthly 'flash' Profit and Loss results

£000s	*Jan Actual*	*Jan Budget*	*Variance*	*YTD 10 mths*	*Budget 10 mths*	*Variance*
Gross fees	***150.00***			***1,650.00***		
Non-recoverable sub-consultants' fees	*-10.00*			*-100.00*		
Net fees	***140.00***	***165.00***	***-25.00***	***1,550.00***	***1,500.00***	***50.00***
Resource costs	*85.00*	*90.00*	*5.00*	*950.00*	*800.00*	*-150.00*
Overheads	*42.00*	*40.00*	*-2.00*	*385.00*	*400.00*	*15.00*
Net profit before tax	***13.00***	***35.00***	***-22.00***	***215.00***	***300.00***	***-85.00***

Monthly flash Profit and Loss results

This report is a condensed summary of the Profit and Loss account. It shows what profit has been made in the month that is being reported and what the resulting cumulative position is year to date (YTD). Both are then compared with the budget. It gives a high-level overview of the position and allows quick identification of which areas of the practice are missing their targets and experiencing problems.

The flash report shows the performance in the month just gone, plus the financial YTD each in comparison with the original budget. The differences between the *actual* and the *budget* are shown in the *variances* column. Variances are expressed following the usual convention that a positive value is a 'good news' figure, such as higher income than expected or lower expenses, and a negative value shows 'bad news' such as a shortage of income or an overrun on expenses.

The monthly report focuses on just a few key elements so that you can see immediately which area, if any, is causing a problem:

- **Income:** This is shown after allowing for the fees that are being collected for other members of the design team. It is important to ensure that you are only looking at the practice's own net fee income. You must ensure that you are not seduced into complacency by a healthy-looking turnover figure that is 'flattered' by the inclusion of fees that do not really belong to the practice.
- **Resources**: This includes all of the expenses that relate to people. As well as the direct payroll costs, this should include the add-on employer's costs such as National Insurance Contributions (NICs), the cost of benefit plans such as life cover and medical insurance and the cost of continuous professional development (CPD) programmes and recruitment.
- **Overheads**: This sweeps up all of the other categories of expense into one large pot. It is very easy to get bogged down in the detail when it comes to overhead costs. It is of course important to review overheads from time to time to ensure that money is not being wasted. However, it's unlikely that a significant financial problem in an architectural practice is simply the result of spending too much on overheads. It is far more likely to be a structural issue such as the wrong number or the wrong mix of staff for the work on hand. It is all too easy to avoid facing up to these difficult issues by getting immersed in finding the reasons for a minor overspend on stationery or telephone charges.

The flash report enables you to quickly assimilate if the practice is making a profit or not, where you stand in relation to the budget and whether this is a temporary problem or more of a long-term issue.

In the example shown I would initially observe that net profit for the current month of January was only just over a third of its budgeted target (i.e. £13,000 for pre-tax profit compared with a predicted £35,000). A look at the *variances* shows that this was largely due to a shortfall in fees of £25,000.

Although there was a saving on resource costs and a small overspend on overheads this did not affect the overall picture. The question to address is why were the fees less than expected?

Any movements in 'work in progress' (WIP) are deliberately left out of this report: firstly, because it would slow down the process to work out the change in WIP from month to month; and secondly, because it encourages the practice to remain focused on getting invoices out to clients for the work completed.

Thus, in the example it could well be that the work has been done but the practice has not managed to get the relevant invoice issued before the month-end accounting cut-off, in which case this variance should rectify itself in the following month.

Turning to the cumulative YTD picture, which in the example is at the 10 months point, a different story emerges. Again, starting at the bottom line, you can see that there is a serious pre-tax profit shortfall of £85,000 (£300,000 minus £215,000). But the reasons are different. The variance analysis shows that the practice is actually ahead on fees in the year but has seriously overspent on people costs. There have been some modest savings in the overhead area. Perhaps this issue has already been addressed; the current month figures would seem to suggest that it has, but it does now seem that the financial year will not achieve the profit level that was budgeted, because there are now only two months to go.

KEY PERFORMANCE INDICATORS

To help with the rapid comprehension of the current financial position I recommend that you track a number of profitability key performance indicators (KPIs) each month at your performance management meeting as follows:

Key performance indicators

Profitability indicators	*This month Actual*	*This month Budget*	*Bench-mark*	*YTD Actual*	*YTD Budget*	*Bench-mark*
Turnover by director (£000s)	35	40	30	36	40	30
Turnover per fee earner (£000s)	4.5	6	5	4.8	6	5
Profit as % of turnover	12	15	15	11	15	15
Profit per director (£000s)	4.8	5	5	4.6	5	5
Profit per fee earner (£000s)	1.8	2	1	1.6	2	1
Liquidity indicators						
Overdraft cover				3.5	2	2
Current ratio				1.4	1	1
Quick/Acid test ratio				1.2	1	1

KPIs
This chart summarises the key measures of financial performance and compares them with the practice's own budget and an industry benchmark. Figures are shown for the current month and YTD. The first five measures are concerned with income and profit; the final indicator is a measure of liquidity often quoted in bank overdraft agreements.

- **Turnover by director/partner**: This is a broad indicator of how much business the average director is managing on an annual basis. In our practice we aim for an annual turnover of £500,000 per director. This means that with four directors we would expect annual net architectural turnover of £2 million.
- **Turnover per fee earner**: This is very similar to the director/partner turnover KPI above. We look for a turnover of £100,000 per fee earner per year.
- **Profit per director/partner**: This KPI looks at the bottom line and works out how much pre-tax profit is being made per director. On a projected turnover of £2 million we would aim for a 12.5 per cent pre-tax profit which is £250,000 which equates to an average profit of £62,500 per director.
- **Profit per fee earner**: This again mirrors the director equivalent above. We would look for a profit of £15,000 per fee earner.

Each of these KPIs can be compared with the budgeted values and also to the benchmarks published by the RIBA inter-firm comparison.

As with all ratio analysis, the use of KPIs is at its most useful when viewed in terms of a trend rather than in isolation. Circumstances may conspire to make the position at the end of a particular month unrepresentative of the general pattern. Looking at a particular KPI's performance over a 9- or 12-month period will eliminate this sort of short-term anomaly.

LIQUIDITY KPIS

For most practices there will not be any need to produce a full detailed set of accounts (i.e. Profit and Loss account and Balance Sheet) every month. The Profit and Loss account shows how the practice performed over a period of time, usually the 12-month period that comprises the financial year. The Balance Sheet is a picture of the business as it exists at a particular moment in time, usually at the end of the annual Profit and Loss period. For example, if the financial year runs for 12 months from 1 April to the following 31 March, then the Profit and Loss account is expressed as being for the 12-month period ending 31 March, whereas our Balance Sheet just shows the closing position as at 31 March.

The Balance Sheet is often analysed in terms of the ratios between its different elements. This sort of analysis enables you to see how much the business runs on borrowed money rather than the money invested or retained from the profits of previous years. In particular, it shows whether there is a liquidity problem (i.e. will the business have the cash available to pay its bills as they become due).

It is possible to carry out this sort of analysis from the sort of information that is usually readily available to most practices. For example, in my practice, we have developed liquidity KPIs which we review each month along with the profitability KPIs described above, as follows:

OVERDRAFT COVER

Overdraft cover is a measure that is favoured by many banks, and is often written into overdraft agreements as a condition of the continuation of the facility (known as a bank covenant).

The usual requirement is for a minimum overdraft cover of two times the overdraft limit.

However, it is worth noting that the debtor value used in this calculation needs to be restricted to genuinely recoverable amounts. Many businesses tend to leave unpaid invoice balances on their aged debtor list for many years. Although this can be a useful way of keeping them in mind, it does overstate the amount that the practice can realistically expect to collect. I prefer to keep the aged debtor list as clean as possible and either actively pursue the outstanding debt or acknowledge that it is a dead loss and to write it off.

CURRENT RATIO

The current ratio is a liquidity and efficiency ratio that measures a firm's ability to pay off its short-term liabilities with its current assets. The current ratio is an important measure of liquidity because short-term liabilities are due within the next year.

This means that a practice has a limited amount of time in order to raise the funds to pay for these liabilities. Companies with larger amounts of current assets will more easily be able to pay off current liabilities when they become due without having to sell off long-term income-generating assets.

The current ratio is calculated by dividing current assets by current liabilities, as shown opposite.

WORKED EXAMPLE: OVERDRAFT COVER

Overdraft cover = Amount owed by clients (debtors)

Overdraft balance

If, at the end of the month, total amount due from clients = £225,000 and overdraft balance = £90,000

then overdraft cover = $\frac{225,000}{90,000}$ **= 2.5**

In this example, the overdraft cover is 2.5, which is more than double (2 times) the overdraft limit and therefore would be considered satisfactory.

WORKED EXAMPLE: CURRENT RATIO

$$\text{Current ratio} = \frac{\text{current assets}}{\text{current liabilities}}$$

If current assets = petty cash + bank balance + debts + WIP

= £500 + £20,000 + £100,000 + £75,000 = £195,500

and current liabilities = short term liabilities of payroll, bank overdraft and short-term loans, taxes and suppliers = £150,000

$$\text{then current ratio} = \frac{195{,}000}{150{,}000} = 1.30$$

In this example, the current ratio is 1.30, which is above 1 and therefore would be considered satisfactory.

Clearly, the higher the value of the current ratio the better and this is an indicator of how much the practice is operating on a 'hand-to-mouth' basis.

THE QUICK RATIO OR ACID TEST

The quick ratio (or acid test ratio) is a liquidity ratio that measures the ability of a company to pay its current liabilities when they come due using only 'quick' assets. Quick assets are current assets that can be converted to cash within the short-term, which is usually defined as within 90 days. Cash in the bank, petty cash on hand and the amounts owed by our clients (debtors) are considered to be quick assets.

WORKED EXAMPLE: QUICK RATIO (ACID TEST RATIO)

$$\text{Quick ratio} = \frac{\text{cash + current account bank balance + debts}}{\text{current liabilities}}$$

Taking the same values used in the previous example:

petty cash + bank balance + debts

= £500 + £20,000 + £100,000 = £120,500

and

short-term liabilities of payroll, taxes and suppliers = £95,000

$$\text{then quick ratio} = \frac{120{,}500}{95{,}000} = 1.27$$

In this example, the quick ratio is 1.27, which is above 1 and therefore would be considered satisfactory.

The quick ratio is often called the acid test ratio in reference to the historical use of acid to test metals for gold by the early miners. If the metal passed the acid test, it was pure gold. If metal failed the acid test by corroding from the acid, it was a base metal and of no value.

The acid test of finance shows how well a company can quickly convert its assets into cash in order to pay off its current liabilities. It also shows the level of quick assets to current liabilities.

It is increasingly common to see these liquidity ratios being used as KPIs in public sector pre-qualification questionnaires. If a practice fails these simple balance sheet analysis tests their application to work on the project is eliminated immediately before any consideration is given to their architectural skills or experience. A ratio of less than 1 is taken as a sign of financial fragility, which the commissioning body considers to be too great a risk to the fulfilment of the project overall.

SUMMARY

- The financial manager needs to look ahead and predict what the financial future holds for the practice. The accounting process aims to provide an accurate picture of the current financial position of the practice.
- A sound book-keeping system that is simple to use and keep up to date is essential.
- There is a difference between producing figures for management purposes and producing data to satisfy the legal requirements of HMRC and Companies House. The emphasis in the production of management information is on the speed of reporting, so a degree of estimation is acceptable as long as the overall impression is accurate.
- The aim of management information is to facilitate rapid action to remedy a situation before it develops into too great a problem.
- Accurate figures for income and outgoings on people and property provide a fairly good picture of the profitability of the practice in that period of time.
- KPIs can be used to assess quickly which areas, if any, are a problem and need to be addressed.
- KPIs cover not just measures of turnover and profits but also of financing and liquidity. Each practice can evolve its own KPIs to suit its particular market and organisational needs.

PLANNING THE FINANCIAL HEALTH OF THE PRACTICE

With the accounting foundations in place so that you know where you are and how you got here, you can then have the confidence to turn your attention to the future. Armed with the knowledge of the practice's past performance you can start to decide what you would like to have happen next.

It is important to have a long-term strategic and financial plan and to allow your thinking to break free occasionally from the tyranny of the accounting year. Although the 12-month financial period is a natural and convenient period of time to use, it can result in an unhealthy focus on the short-term view which is particularly out of step with the long-term nature of construction and architecture.

DEVELOPING A STRATEGIC PLAN

Many studies have concluded that there is a strong correlation between those businesses that are financially successful and those where the management team have taken the time to develop and share a vision of where the business will be in five or ten years' time. The practice that has worked out what it has to offer that is special or different, and has identified the sort of client who would be attracted by what differentiates it from the competition, has already gone a long way to increasing its chances of being a success. Thus the annual budget process needs to be preceded by the development of a five-year plan.

The five-year plan needs to define the strategic objectives for the business, and then express them year by year as a series of measurable targets or benchmarks that can be kept under review. That which can be measured can be monitored and managed.

Many people seem reluctant to engage with this process and find it difficult to escape from the 'noise' of the day-to-day workload. It can seem like an indulgence to take time out of the working week for blue sky thinking and debate.

There is a degree of fear when we ask ourselves to look beyond the immediate future: we all fear the potential embarrassment of setting out a grand plan and then publicly failing to achieve it. Yet those who undertake this sort of exercise regularly are convinced of its benefits.
People also seem to lose sight of the fact that even when the exercise is complete, bound and published it is still only a plan. The plan should not be abandoned at the first sight of trouble, but equally you are not bound by it and the plan can (and should) be revisited and revised in the light of experience.

It is a worthwhile exercise to define the direction in which you expect the practice to go. In the absence of this there is a strong possibility that you will be taken in whatever direction events happen to lead.

THE ANNUAL BUDGET

Having settled on a five-year strategic plan, you are now ready to tackle the budget for the coming year.

It is logical to use the actual results of the previous financial year as a starting point, but it is also important to ensure that you do not carry forward and build in errors and patterns from the past. Equally, many expense budgets are prepared by simply adding an inflation factor to

WORKED EXAMPLE: FIVE-YEAR PLAN

Strategic objectives

- **To double the size of the practice**
- **To improve profitability**
- **To expand into the healthcare sector.**

	Current	Year 1	Year 2	Year 3	Year 4	Year 5
Sales (£million)	*£1.2*	*£1.5*	*£1.8*	*£2.0*	*£2.2*	*£2.4*
Profit	*£75,000*	*£105,000*	*£144,000*	*£180,000*	*£220,000*	*£240,000*
Pre-tax profit (%)	*6%*	*7%*	*8%*	*9%*	*10%*	*10%*
Qualified staff	*10*	*12*	*14*	*16*	*18*	*20*
Healthcare as % of sales	*5%*	*7%*	*9%*	*10%*	*12%*	*12%*

This is a manageable number of targets to monitor and the annual feedback report should give a clear indication of progress.

last year's value. This is easy, but not always a helpful or intelligent way to approach the exercise. This approach may apply to some routine items such as utility costs, but it is dangerous to simply apply it across the board.

ZERO-BASED BUDGETS

It is a good idea to go through a zero-based budget exercise every few years. This approach involves taking a critical line by line review of every expenditure and asking these questions:

› Do we really need to spend this money?

› What would the implications be if we did not spend this money?

› Is there another way to achieve the same result that we get from our current expenditure?

This can be a difficult but rewarding exercise. In general, architectural practices do not invest the time in the budget process that it deserves, and consequently they do not get the benefits from it that they could.

For example, consider the amount spent on the office rent. Surely this is a fixed cost? Well, it probably is in the short to medium term, but try asking the zero-based questions and see where it leads:

› Do we really need an office of this size?

› Does it really need to be in this location?

› Is there scope for people to work more remotely or from home?

› Do we use the available technology to make home working as easy as possible?

› Could hot-desking work for us?

› Could we make more use of teleconferencing for meetings?

› Could we outsource some of our work – either to smaller local practices or overseas?

› Why are we renting when we could be buying (or vice versa)?

This can be a liberating intellectual process that forces you to consider how that practice really operates and how you would like to see it develop.

IDENTIFYING THE KEY LIMITING FACTOR

Having established the turnover and profit targets for the coming year and five-year plan, the next task is to focus on identifying the one area that is most likely to make it difficult for our plans to be achieved. This is often referred to as the key limiting factor.

It's easy to assume that this factor will be the level of sales (i.e. can the practice win and deliver enough work to be able to invoice clients at the income level we are targeting?). But other factors can also be involved. For example, in the architecture sector some practices are limited by the availability of people with the right skills and experience for the project work in hand; other practices may be limited primarily by lack of space or computer equipment or software.

It is important to identify the limiting factor because it provides a starting point for the budget process. For example, assume that the limiting factor is a shortage of people with the right skills. How might you address this problem? You would need to budget for expenditure on recruitment, advertising or agency fees but – probably more importantly – you also need to budget the time that current staff will need to spend interviewing and administering the recruitment activity. (Architectural practices need to budget staff time carefully because this is the key resource and staff time is essentially all that the practice has to sell.) In addition, you need to allow time for marketing activities and professional training and development. A number of the senior people in the practice will have a variety of responsibilities for managing the practice and this, too, has to be taken into account. However, you also need to ensure that across the practice overall there is enough time available to deliver the required level of project work to an appropriate standard.

THE BUDGET-SETTING PROCESS

Budgets work best when key personnel in the practice have a sense of ownership of the final result. Budgets that are imposed without any consultation by a remote management team are likely to be resented and resisted.

The budget-setting process should begin with the various individuals or groups in the practice being invited to make a budget proposal of what they would like to spend in their area and why.

At SEH we have formed a variety of special interest groups, for example a group focused on the issue of sustainability, and another group focused on the use of technology. We have been keen to encourage administrative and support staff to be a part of these groups and to bring their own unique perspective to their architect colleagues. We invite each of these groups to a budget review meeting where their ideas can be discussed and where they can present the 'business case' for the money that they would like the practice to spend. It must, however, be clear from the outset that these can only be proposals until the budget is finalised. It is frequently the case that, when you add together all the proposals for expenditure from the various budget holders, they total 150 per cent or more of the available funds.

The financial manager's job is to reconcile the top-down approach that comes from the targets of the financial year derived from the five-year plan, with a bottom-up approach that comes from the individual budget holders or groups. The identification of the limiting factor helps when deciding where the practice's efforts, resources and money can best be used.

Once the process has been completed, it is important that each person or group involved receives feedback on their budget submission. They will need to understand why their submission has been approved or amended in the context of the overall budget for the year. Hopefully, they'll be able to appreciate how their individual budget fits into the goals of the practice as a whole.

CONTROLLING THE BUDGET

The budget for the year effectively becomes an authority to spend the money that has been approved. As expenditure arises it should be approved by the appropriate budget

Annual budget for the 12 months ending (date)	Budget (£000s)	Previous year Actual (£000s)	Previous year Budget (£000s)
Gross architecture fees	£2,500	£2,355	£2,400
Other income	£15	£12	£-
Total income	***£2,515***	***£2,367***	***£2,400***
less			
Sub-consultant costs	£125	£115	£50
Net income	***£2,390***	***£2,252***	***£2,350***
Project-related resource costs	£1,250	£1,305	£1,275
Non-project-related resource costs	£355	£400	£300
Total: resource costs	***£1,605***	***£1,705***	***£1,575***
Other expenditure			
Property costs	£225	£215	£210
Office costs	£275	£300	£275
Insurance incl. PII	£40	£45	£45
Travel and entertainment	£50	£55	£35
Advertising and promotion	£45	£40	£45
Legal and professional fees	£25	£20	£25
Other expenses	£15	£15	£15
Total: other expenditure	***£675***	***£690***	***£650***
Operating profit (pre-tax)	***£110***	***-£143***	***£125***
Interest costs or income	£15	£20	£16
Profit before tax	***£95***	***-£163***	***£109***
Corporation tax (at, say, 20%)	£22	-£29	£25
Profit after tax	***£88***	***-£114***	***£100***

Annual budget
This is an example of an annual operating budget. It shows the amount of profit which the practice plans to make in the year and compares this year with both the previous year's actual performance and the original budget for the previous year.

holder before it is processed for payment. The budget holder should also receive regular feedback, perhaps once a quarter, showing what they have spent in their area and how this compares with the budget. This gives the budget holder the opportunity to make changes so that their activity comes in on budget at the end of the financial year.

However, there is a danger that, if the level of overall activity is far greater or less than was anticipated, the approved levels of budgeted expenditure will no longer 'fit'. This means that there is a need to review the actual financial results on a quarterly basis and decided if there is a need to 'flex' or adjust the budget accordingly. It is clearly going to be a problem to maintain expenditure at the agreed level if fee income is 25 per cent lower than was anticipated. Equally, however, it would be problematic to maintain the original budgeted level of expenditure when monthly income is 25 per cent higher than was expected. This is very likely to require some support in the form of extra spend.

These periodic adjustments should be a fine-tuning exercise rather than a repeat of the whole process. Don't simply abandon the original budget; instead, update it as the year progresses with refinements in selected areas as required.

CAPITAL EXPENDITURE BUDGETS

For accounting purposes, a distinction is drawn between revenue expenditure and general expenditure. Capital expenditure is the money spent on items that are long term in nature and will remain in the business longer than the current financial year. Examples of capital items are vehicles, furniture and computer equipment.

In an architectural practice (and in many other businesses) there is an ongoing need to upgrade or replace computers to ensure that they can operate increasingly sophisticated drawing and three-dimensional modelling software as it is developed. Failure to have the most up-to-date software available, for example, to be able to operate building information modelling (BIM), could pose a serious threat to a practice's ability to compete for work.

Clients have ever-rising levels of expectation when it comes to the quality of presentation and visualisation material provided by their architects. What was considered to be cutting edge technology two years ago is now simply the expected standard. If a practice fails to employ the latest techniques that others are using in their competitive presentations, clients will notice and draw their own conclusions about the practice's capabilities. Modern software requires an ever-increasing amount of electronic storage space. This means that money needs to be spent regularly on servers and back-up facilities. This expenditure needs to be included in the budget.

Example capital expenditure budget for the year ending 31 March	
Proposed spend in the year:	
IT equipment	
Projector for client presentations	*£2,000.00*
3 new printers	*£3,600.00*
Graphics card upgrades	*£3,000.00*
7 new computers – rolling update programme	*£11,900.00*
Expand capacity of email server	*£5,500.00*
Sub-total	***£26,000.00***
Office improvements	
Reception area upgrade	*£2,000.00*
Replace entrance screen	*£2,000.00*
Kitchen refurbishmnet	*£3,000.00*
Office lighting improvement	*£2,500.00*
Sub-total	***£9,500.00***
Total	***£35,500.00***

Capital expenditure
This chart shows the amount of money that the practice has agreed to devote to long-term expenditure. The items detailed are not included as expenses in the annual Profit and Loss account because they will have an ongoing value to the business for several years. The value of each item is charged gradually to the Profit and Loss account for a number of years in the form of 'depreciation'.

One of the key reasons for making an adequate level of profit is to provide the funding for this sort of reinvestment in the business.

Capital expenditure budgets are often prepared on a medium- to long-term basis (i.e. on a rolling three- to five-year basis). From this plan the capital expenditure for the coming financial year can be agreed and integrated into the budgeting process. Although expenditure on capital equipment does not immediately affect the profit recorded in the year, other than in the depreciation charge, it will have a significant impact on the cash flow forecast (which is discussed in Chapter 7).

It is worth noting that depreciation is not recognised as an expense when it comes to the calculation of income tax or corporation tax. Instead, the tax system allows businesses to claim a variety of capital allowances each year. For example, for some time there has been the generous level of 100 per cent first-year allowances on plant and machinery, which includes items such as computer equipment. This means that, at the time of writing, the whole cost of qualifying capital expenditure can be claimed as an expense in the year in which it was incurred, and this of course serves to reduce the taxable profit in that year accordingly. The reduction in taxable profit, of course, carries through to a reduction in the tax bill.

BUDGETS FOR THE SOLE PRACTITIONER OR SMALL PRACTICE

People working in a small practice or perhaps on their own may be wondering how they can apply these ideas. As with all of the tools and methods described in this book, the underlying principles remain the same, regardless of the size of the practice. I feel that even the smallest of practices could benefit from having some version of all the tools and reports described. Judgement is needed, of course, in deciding how to scale and adapt each of the particular techniques to suit the individual small practice.

I would certainly recommend that every practice - even sole practitioners - should set aside some time to work out and write down a three- or five-year strategic plan, and then to produce a budget for the coming year accordingly. I believe it is important to end up with a written plan and budget because this forces us all to be clearer and more decisive in our thinking. The plan is more 'real' when it has a physical form.

It is always a fascinating exercise to go back to an earlier statement of intent, plan or budget and compare that with what actually happened.

The budget provides a map of the financial journey ahead and a point of reference for comparison purposes along the way. The pay-off for investing your time in this process comes when the comparisons to the plan or budget prompt you to ask questions you might otherwise not have asked which, in turn, is more likely to lead you to the real source of the problem than simply relying on gut feelings or instincts, which are coloured by preconceptions or prejudices.

SUMMARY

› Successful businesses of any kind usually have a strategic, long-term plan and the management team shares a vision of what and where the business will be in five or even ten years' time. This is then translated into a rolling five-year business plan.

› The annual budget, which describes what is going to happen in the coming 12 months, is derived from the five-year plan.

› It can be useful to adopt a zero-based approach to the budget process every few years. This challenging exercise starts by taking nothing for granted and asking whether each of the items of expenditure is really necessary and worthwhile.

› Identify the key limiting factor for the practice: the single most important element that will determine whether it will be successful in achieving budget targets. Examples of limiting factors include: ability to achieve the projected level of sales; and whether the practice has the correct mix of people, or sufficient office space or technological resources.

- Budgets should be kept under review on a quarterly or half-yearly basis.
- It may be necessary to adjust the budget when business activity has been higher or lower than originally predicted.
- Large-scale capital expenditure should be planned and integrated into the overall budget and future cash flow process.

04

PROJECT REPORTING

PROJECT REPORTING AND CONTROL

The ultimate aim in the management of an architectural practice is to ensure that the practice always has the financial resources in place that will allow the architects to do the sort of design work that they would choose to do. The practice must make sufficient overall profit to be self-sustaining. The best way to ensure this is to monitor the performance of each project as it progresses. By adopting the discipline of planning the financial targets of each new project as it comes in to the office, and then comparing its performance to what was planned, there is a far better chance of achieving the desired overall result.

However, it is often quite difficult to capture all of the necessary financial information at the outset of a new project. Still elated from having won the assignment in the first place, the team are naturally enthusiastic to 'get stuck in' to the design process and not to worry about what may seem to be peripheral paperwork. So this is one of those occasions when it is necessary to introduce the tension between the design process and financial reality which I described in the Introduction. If you don't ensure at the outset that you know what the practice can expect to get paid for this project, and what needs to be spent to earn this fee, then there is a significant chance that you will reach the end of the project with only a vague sense of whether the project was financially worthwhile.

It is essential that the time is taken to think through the project plan in terms of what resources will be needed for each stage and for how long. This can then by translated into a cost plan by work stage against which you can monitor actual performance. You need to know from the beginning:

- How much is the overall fee?
- Are there other members of the design team that need to be paid from this fee (e.g. engineers or quantity surveyors)?
- Is there an agreed fee schedule?
- Is there a detailed resource plan that shows who is allocated to the project on a week by week and stage by stage basis?
- Are there significant other expenses involved (such as travel, hotel or printing costs) that will need to be absorbed as a part of the fee?

If this does not exist, the financial manager must risk unpopularity by continuing to ask for the information until they receive it. Once the information materialises, you can use it to develop a financial performance model that can be used to monitor the project as it develops.

THE CALCULATION OF COST

The largest cost on a project of any size will be the architectural resources used – that is, the cost of the people working on the job. This may of course also include architectural services that are being bought in on a temporary or contract basis.

Architects are paid on a time basis – an annual salary is essentially a contract to purchase a package of professional hours over the course of a year. So the logical measure of the cost of resources is a time-based calculation, and for this to work it is crucial to have a robust time-recording system.

The detailed recording of time is one of those administrative activities that does not come easily to many architects. The advent of electronic time recording systems has made the process much easier in recent years. Yet in any practice, it seems that there will always be about 10 per cent of the staff who are always late in submitting their timesheets (and expenses). This is not restricted to architects by the way; every professional services firm encounters the same issue.

I have tried a wide variety of strategies to encourage these few miscreants to come into line: neither carrot nor stick seem particularly effective. The most workable solution that I have used is an automated reminder system, backed up with tenacity and a sense of humour. It is, however, essential for the integrity of the costing system that all time is properly recorded as soon as possible.

I am always concerned that there is a disconnection in the mind of the architect between the time they are spending on a project and the eventual profitability of that project. When the final reckoning comes there is often an element of surprise that the financial result for the project is disappointing. In my experience working with solicitors and accountants, who are usually obliged to record their time in six-minute units, there is a much greater awareness that time really is money.

WORKED EXAMPLE:
ANNUAL COSTS FOR EMPLOYING ONE STAFF MEMBER

Base salary	*£36,000*
Employer's NICs	*£4,165*
RIBA/ARB subscriptions	*£300*
Employer's Pension Contribution	*£1,200*
Life insurance premium	*£150*
Health insurance premium	*£300*
Total	***£42,115***

To arrive at the appropriate hourly rate for this staff member, you need to calculate the number of hours available for work in a year.

The general standard is to assume that there are 220 working days per year (i.e. excluding weekends, statutory holidays and, say, five weeks of paid leave) in a year, which equals 44 working weeks. If staff work a standard 35-hour week that is 1,540 hours per year.

Thus the calculation of the direct cost for this person would be:

£42,115 divided by 1,540 hours = £27.35 per hour.

The use of modern fully integrated project management and accounting software should make the financial position of each individual project and the practice overall much easier to track. However, there still seems to be a reluctance to engage fully with the process of keeping the information in the software up to date or to abandon the imperfect home-made tools such as spreadsheets. As an accountant, I am a great fan of the spreadsheet and use them extensively in my work every day. However, I am also aware that there comes a point where the amount of manipulation of data required is beyond the scope of the spreadsheet – or more accurately, beyond the skill level of the spreadsheet user. This is the point at which to acknowledge that project accounting software is going to be a worthwhile investment of time and money.

The practice finance manager needs to develop a direct cost rate for each person expressed in terms of £ per hour. The direct cost calculation needs to encompass not just the base salary and any regular overtime payments, if applicable, but also the add-on costs of benefits and employer's national insurance contributions (NICs). Note, however, that this is only the cost of employing the person – it is not the same as the charge-out rate.

This direct cost calculation should be performed for each member of staff. Note, however, that problems can arise if individual rates are published, because there may be a close correlation with the underlying salary, so pay differentials could be accidentally exposed. To avoid this problem, I recommend that a standard average cost rate is used that applies to groups of people rather than individuals (e.g.'all Part 3 students are costed at £20 per hour per person'). These rates will, of course, need to be recalculated when salaries change during the year.

The direct cost calculation uses only the elements that comprise the remuneration package, which is why it is termed the *direct cost*.

It is also possible to add in an allowance for a share of the office overheads, which are known as *indirect costs*. The overheads allowance can be calculated in a variety of ways, but is often derived by dividing the total overhead costs of the practice by the total number of planned chargeable hours. Thus, if all of the fee-earning staff performed the planned number of chargeable hours, then all the costs of the practice would be recovered.

Other than for the very smallest practices I prefer not to include indirect costs when working out the cost of employing staff, because the calculation of these charges (i.e. the non-staff overheads of the business) can be difficult and, since the calculation is constantly changing, the results can be misleading. I would recommend the simpler 'contribution costing' approach.

The contribution costing approach does not account for the non-staff overheads; instead we identify the 'profit' of each project by looking

Project resource plan

	Hours	***Jan***	***Feb***	***Mar***
Director		*50*	*40*	*40*
Associate		*95*	*125*	*125*
Architect		*290*	*350*	*350*
Assistant architect		*400*	*500*	*500*
Total		***835***	***1015***	***1015***

	Cost rate per hour	***Jan***	***Feb***	***Mar***
Director	*£50*	*£2,500*	*£2,000*	*£2,000*
Associate	*£40*	*£3,800*	*£5,000*	*£5,000*
Architect	*£30*	*£8,700*	*£10,500*	*£10,500*
Assistant architect	*£25*	*£10,000*	*£12,500*	*£12,500*
Total		***£25,000***	***£30,000***	***£30,000***
Cumulative total		***£25,000***	***£55,000***	***£85,000***

only at the direct resource costs, as calculated in the example above. That amount is deducted from the final fee, and the result equates to the contribution of that particular project to the rest of the overheads of the office. Applying this approach to all projects is an excellent aid to decision-making, because it means you can easily check, over the course of a financial year, whether the projects in hand/completed are making a contribution that is sufficient to cover the overheads and provide the desired level of overall profit.

As already mentioned, the direct cost is different from the charge-out rate. Charge-out rates should include an allowance for indirect costs, non-fee-earning time (i.e. practice administration, marketing, training) and also provide for a project profit margin.

Armed with the data on total cost of all the employees, you can now work up a detailed project resource plan, as shown in the following examples.

Project resource plan

This spreadsheet shows the number of hours of each grade of person that will be needed on a month by month basis. The hours are translated into a cost by multiplying by the appropriate direct cost rate, as shown in the second half of the sheet.

Apr	*May*	*Jun*	*Jul*	*Aug*	*Sept*
5	*24*	*25*	*50*	*5*	*2*
55	*95*	*50*	*95*	*55*	*8*
200	*500*	*350*	*290*	*200*	*76*
262	*600*	*250*	*400*	*262*	*92*
522	***1219***	***675***	***835***	***522***	***178***

Apr	*May*	*Jun*	*Jul*	*Aug*	*Sept*
£250	*£1,200*	*£1,250*	*£2,500*	*£250*	*£100*
£2,200	*£3,800*	*£2,000*	*£3,800*	*£2,200*	*£320*
£6,000	*£15,000*	*£10,500*	*£8,700*	*£6,000*	*£2,280*
£6,550	*£15,000*	*£6,250*	*£10,000*	*£6,550*	*£2,300*
£15,000	***£35,000***	***£20,000***	***£25,000***	***£15,000***	***£5,000***
£100,000	***£135,000***	***£155,000***	***£180,000***	***£195,000***	***£200,000***

Projected fee and projected contribution (fee minus direct costs)

The values can be plotted onto a graph (as shown below) together with the projected fees. This project performance chart allows us to see how the planned contribution (planned fee minus planned direct cost) builds up over the course of the project.

PROJECTED FEE
PROJECTED COST

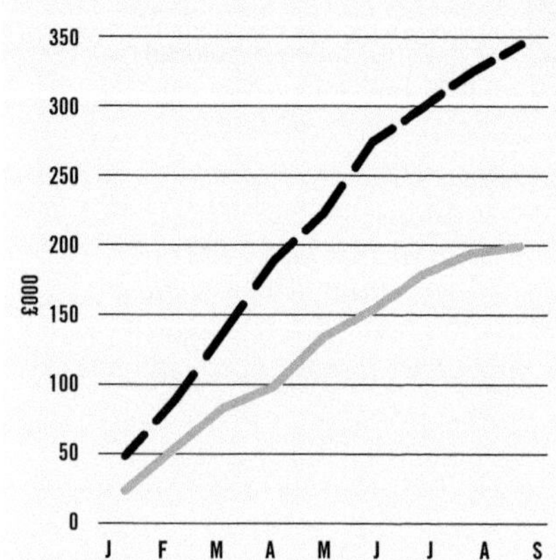

Add in the actual fees

This graph illustrates the same project but with its actual fees now added. From this you can see immediately where the project has deviated from the original plan.

PROJECTED FEE ACTUAL FEE
PROJECTED COST

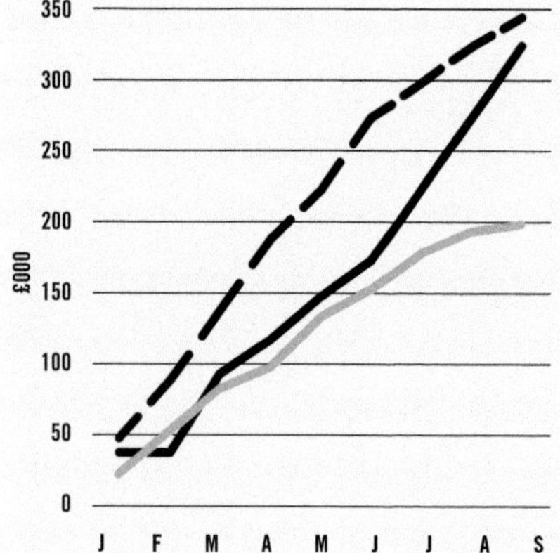

The whole picture: actual fees and actual costs

This final graph completes the picture by adding the actual costs extracted from the time recording system. This theoretical example does not make for happy reading. The final fee has turned out to be less than was originally planned, and the actual costs have turned out to be well over the original estimate. Consequently, the planned contribution of £145,000 has been reduced to an actual contribution of only £75,000.

PROJECTED FEE ACTUAL FEE
PROJECTED COST

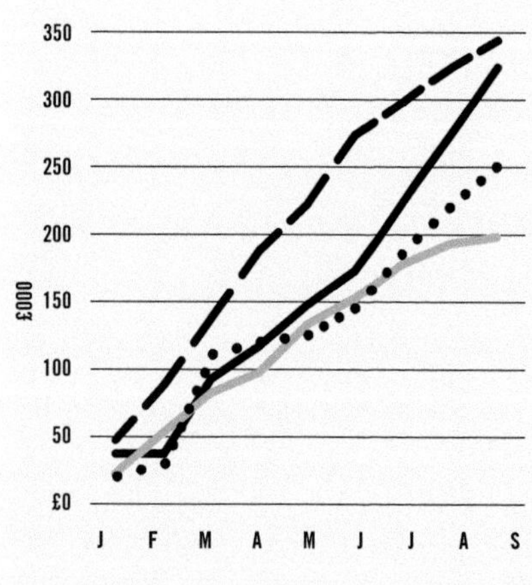

Presenting the information in graphs enables you to see problems quickly as they arise. This should prompt an investigation of the situation until the cause of the deviation is understood. The approach also means that you can review many projects quickly. Hopefully, most will be more or less on track and not require any further attention, and your time can then be spent managing those projects that seem to be going off course.

It is important to note, however, that the graphs show when something is not going to plan, but this does not necessarily mean that things are going wrong. A squeezing of the planned contribution, as demonstrated by the narrowing of the gap between the actual fee and cost lines, is prima facie evidence of a problem. However, it may simply be that the client has expanded the scope of the work and that more people have been working on the project than was originally planned. As long as you pick up this sort of information before it is too late, and negotiate an additional fee for this work, this is potentially good news for the practice.

Over the course of time these project profiles can grow into a useful reference library, building up information so that you can look for patterns and trends. Does the practice experience particularly high or low levels of contribution in particular sectors or types of project? And you may soon learn that it is hard to make good levels of profit on small-scale projects, and profits tend to come from the larger projects. But you may decide to try to ensure that the practice maintains a healthy mixture of both.

Again this can result in tension in practice. A profitable project may well be one that is large in scale and contains a high degree of repetitive tasks or the use of standard room types etc. This type of work may well be seen as 'boring' by those working on the job who would be far more interested in spending their time on working out an interesting design challenge. The needs of the practice need to be managed and balanced with the needs of the individual architect.

Project performance is particularly prone to the effects of practice myth and rumour. I know of a practice that used to have its own 'conventional wisdom' that hotel work was unprofitable and should be avoided. Hotel work was duly turned away for the next few years. Yet when some brave soul undertook to analyse the actual figures of projects that had been completed, it emerged that the work on hotels was of average profitability after all. It is often surprising to discover that projects which 'everybody knows' are unprofitable may not actually turn out to be so, when actual historical data becomes available for analysis.

Every project is different and one of the few things that we can say with certainty is that situations and problems will arise that no one could have imagined at the outset. It is therefore important to have a monitoring tool available so the financial effect of these events can be seen and responded to as rapidly as possible.

I've always encouraged the sharing of project performance information with the team working on the job.

People enjoy the sense of involvement that this brings and allows them to understand how their own activity fits into and affects the project performance overall.

Architects tend to take their work to heart and like to be part of a successful project. If you can provide them with an awareness of the job's ongoing financial status there is far more chance they will align their own performance with the overall needs of the project.

SUMMARY

- Overall practice profitability is only likely to be achieved if individual projects are targeted and monitored. By ensuring that the majority of projects stay on track and deliver the planned contribution there is a far greater chance of ending up with a profitable business.
- Calculate the cost per hour for each person who is working on the job.
- Develop a detailed resource plan that shows the people required and the periods of time when they will be needed. Apply their hourly cost rates to develop an overall cost for the project.
- Monitor the actual performance of the project against the plan as the project progresses.
- Charts or some other form of graphic reporting enable you to quickly pass over those projects that are on course and to concentrate attention on the few that are not.
- Sharing information with the members of the design team gives them a sense of involvement and responsibility and will allow them to align their own actions with the best interests of the project overall.

05 FEE PROPOSALS

FEE PROPOSALS – SETTING A REALISTIC FEE

When Peter Shepheard, Gabi Epstein and Peter Hunter set up the practice where I work (SEH) just after World War II, the whole process of setting fees was much simpler than it is today. The RIBA published recommended fee scales which simply had to be applied, as appropriate, to the project in hand. That approach changed with the outlawing of recommended fee scales under competition law and EU regulations. So the setting of fees is now an area that each practice has to navigate for itself and on a project by project basis.

Getting the fee right and getting paid for all the work done can only be achieved if the practice knows what its services will cost and understands the business risks of the client and the project. Equally important is the value that the practice puts on its own work and the client's perception of the value that is being added by the architect.

Added value is not constant: each project will generate its own benefits and these may be cash returns for a developer, or more abstract benefits such as better facilities for a hospital or school.

Some clients may not want an 'artistic' solution, just cost-effective delivery. Other clients will appreciate the advantages of having both.

Architect's fees have become an emotive as well as a practical issue since the end of the recommended fee scales. There is no entitlement to a particular level of fee. In addition to costs and profit, the fee has to account for the perceived risks of the project.

At the end of the project the client's opinion of the architect will be influenced by the perceived fairness of the fee. Even the most affluent client will expect value for money, in accordance with their own perceptions, and the fee offer is therefore critical to the reputation and the financial well-being of the practice.

As discussed in Chapter 4, the only element of a professional service that can be measured is the time taken to provide it. All the hours in the working day have a price; there is no free time - salaries have to be paid, the costs of running the business have to be met. The crucial management tool in job costing is the timesheet which records the time spent on project work, marketing, management and administration as well as absences for holidays and sickness.

There are several ways to approach the setting of the fee. One would be to use just empirical data gathered from the experience of previous projects. Another approach would be to try to calculate the resource and consequent cost requirements of the project on a stage by stage basis. The ideal solution for most practices is some combination of both of these processes which acts as a form of cross-check.

This chapter describes the various options for calculating fees and making adjustments at various stages of a project.

EMPIRICAL DATA

Practice records are the best source of data when putting together a new fee proposal. Records will hopefully show the details of each commission by building type, and the time spent by each individual with their grade or salary together with an analysis of the resulting profit or loss. The usefulness of this data is enhanced when records are kept on a 'by work stage' basis. All modern project recording and monitoring software will take care of this process automatically.

RIBA FEES CALCULATOR

The RIBA Fees Calculator tool was launched on the RIBA website in April 2015. It has been designed by RIBA Practice Committee members and staff to assist the smaller practice in preparing fee proposals for clients. To use this tool you need to be an existing RIBA member, you can then access it under Member Login/ Chartered Practice Services/ Resources/Fees calculator. If you would like to find out more about accessing this tool or RIBA Membership, please call 0207 307 3686.

The calculator is in the form of a spreadsheet that allows users to build up data on costs per person or grade and then to apply those costs to the amount of time the user has estimated that it will

take to undertake the project. This results in a figure for the total project cost. To this can be added a profit margin and thus a total proposed fee figure is generated.

The RIBA Fees Calculator has very helpful worked examples and some suggested responses to clients' frequently asked questions about fees.

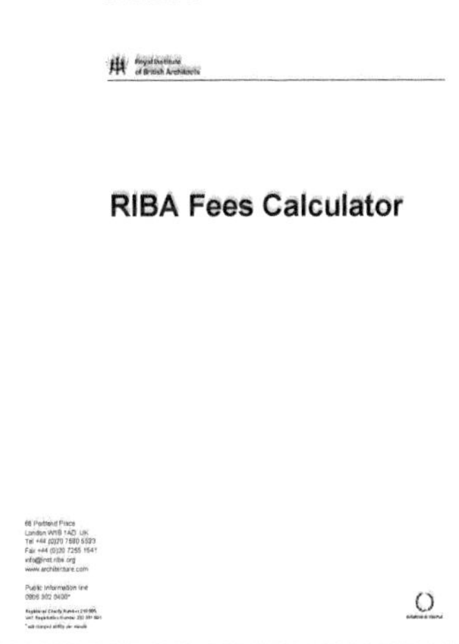

TRADITIONAL APPROACHES TO SETTING FEES

PERCENTAGE FEES

The 'percentage fees' option – which expresses the fee as a percentage of the final cost of construction – is most appropriate for straightforward building projects of relatively short duration, where normal services are required. The details of the project and its cost programme are defined at the beginning. Surveys, feasibility studies, developing the initial brief, and so on would normally involve additional time cost charges.

It is one of the most convenient and easily understood methods of charging, although somewhat rough and ready. This approach also has the problem of appearing to reward the architect for finding ways of increasing the overall construction cost. There is also the opposite risk: that the final construction cost may be lower than was originally anticipated and therefore the resulting architect's fee is less than was planned.

LUMP SUM FEES

Some clients may prefer to agree to a lump sum for the architect's services in advance. It is always desirable to agree such lump sums separately for each work stage, although a single overall lump sum may be divided into appropriate proportions with each section payable on completion of the relevant stage.

The fixed lump sum can work well when the scope of the project, the services required, the programme and cost are clearly defined from the outset, and are likely to remain reasonably stable. However, it would be unwise to agree a fixed sum with no provision for variations except in the case of a highly focused service to be undertaken over a very short period. At the very least, provision should be made for lump sums to be varied if the time or cost parameters changed by more than, say, 10 per cent.

TIME CHARGES

When the resources or the timescale necessary for performance of the architect's services cannot be predicted with reasonable accuracy, time charges will be the best and fairest basis for remuneration. This is particularly relevant to the early stages of the project. The time spent on the relevant services by the various grades of architectural staff is charged at agreed rates usually expressed as £ per hour.

The annual inter-firm comparison report published by the RIBA is a useful source of benchmark hourly rates from other practices in your area (undertaking similar types of work). Other reports on fees are also available from the Fees Bureau.

Whether or not this option is used for the basic fee, always agree rates for appropriate categories of staff and/ or named individuals, as it may be necessary to have agreed rates in place should additional services for extra work become necessary. Provision should be made for revision of the hourly charge rates to take into account inflation at 12-monthly intervals, particularly with services which will be provided over a number of years.

'PERCENTAGE CEILING' FEES

In this method the project proceeds on the basis of a pre-agreed time charge but, if the total fee would exceed an agreed percentage, the latter is applied. The system gives a sort of 'maximum price' relating to the ultimate construction cost. If the hourly rate applies, the client gains but the architect has not lost out, provided that the time charge rates agreed to begin with are realistic and included an allowance for a contribution margin.

UNIT PRICE FEES AND FEES FOR REPETITION

When the project is, or substantial parts of it are, plainly repetitive, fees may be agreed on a unit price basis (e.g. related to the number of hotel rooms, or per house type). The unit price is effectively a form of lump sum.

This approach may also be the basis of a royalty payment for the licence to copy the design on other sites. When a design is to be used on another site or is to be repeated without the involvement of the original architect, for example if a house type is to be repeated by a contractor on various sites, it might be appropriate to agree a licence fee for the use of the architect's work for each house type (see below).

Where the repetition will occur on the original site (e.g. a number of houses or factory units to an identical design), it may be appropriate to adjust the basic fee. The repetitive elements, which will usually occur in the later stages of the project should be acknowledged in setting the fee for those stages at a level that recognises the reduced resources required from the architect.

LICENCE FEES

Whether or not the agreement explicitly says so, the client will have a right to use the architect's work for its intended purpose, for example to construct a building on the identified site, provided that the work has been paid for.

However, if the commission is in any way speculative or at risk from external influences (e.g. in respect of financing or planning), or if it is possible that the client, having obtained the benefit of planning approval, may decide to sell the site or to use the design-and-build approach, the fee offer for the first stages might include an additional premium payment or licence fee for using the work. This fee will become payable if the architect is not appointed to perform further services.

Where it is known that the work will be used for other projects (e.g. producing designs for a house builder), a licence fee or royalty fee for each use should be considered. The amount of that fee will not usually be very significant, although it should include an 'added-value' element.

EXPENSES

Expenses incurred on the project may be:

1. Reimbursed at net cost, perhaps with the addition of an administrative handling charge
2. Reimbursed by a percentage addition to the overall fee
3. Reimbursed by a fixed lump sum
4. Covered by the basic fee.

Option one is simple, but does involve considerable administrative time in collecting the figures and supporting documentation. Option two is simple to operate provided that it is clear to both sides which expenses are intended to be covered by the arrangement. The fixed lump sum (option three) is also easy to operate but does mean that the architect is taking the risk of an expenses overrun. The final option, which in my experience seems to be the most common at the time of writing, means that provision for expenses must be made in the initial calculation of the overall fee agreement. Unrecovered project expenses could make a serious dent in the overall profitability of the project.

The agreement between the practice and the client should make it clear that reimbursement will be due for any expenses not covered by the specified categories if the client's prior approval has been obtained, and for any disbursements made on the client's behalf.

In any event, the architect should record the net cost of all expenses incurred on a project as a part of the project accounting process, because these amounts will need to be taken into account when doing a final project profitability analysis.

FEE ADJUSTMENTS AND CHANGES

The fee may need to be adjusted for any number of reasons, in which case the provisions of the agreement with the client for fee adjustments will be particularly important.

Forms of appointment, such as those published by the RIBA, will provide for remunerating an architect (or practice) involved in extra work or expense. Beware bespoke contracts which limit payment strictly to additional services only if they arise from the client's instruction. Wise architects will always notify the client as soon as they become aware that additional services are going to be required.

An agreed procedure to record changes to the service or completed design information will provide a proper basis for claims for additional or adjusted fees to be made. On a small project this may be achieved by the use of a different form of coding on timesheet records. For larger projects it may be appropriate to establish a procedure of 'change control' requiring all proposed changes affecting other parties to be notified, approved and recorded together with the cost consequences including fees, the source of the change, the relevant date and an identifying reference number.

The following examples explain when adjustments might be justifiably claimed in addition to the basic fee.

REVISION TO BRIEF OR CLIENT'S INSTRUCTIONS

If a client for a planned new office building decides to move their accounts department to another building and replace it with a design studio, additional fees would be due on a time basis (or, if appropriate, an agreed lump sum), until the revised requirements are incorporated into the design. At this point the basic fee arrangement will apply based on the updated cost of construction. In the case of fixed lump sums, there may be a case to argue that the subsequent sums should be adjusted, if the original agreement allows.

ACCELERATION

If the client decides to modify the timetable to achieve earlier occupation, the practice may need to review budgets and time charges, or might opt to agree a fixed lump sum for each work stage affected. These adjustments should be based on best estimates taking into account that:

- Additional resources may be required, perhaps including overtime working
- Some works might be covered by provisional measurement or sums requiring design information to be prepared or modified during the construction period
- The contract administration period will be reduced, although the volume of construction work would remain the same.

The biggest difficulty may be in agreeing the exact starting point from which additional resources would become chargeable.

OMISSION OF WORK IN THE ORIGINAL BRIEF OR COST OF CONSTRUCTION

The initial fee calculation will be based on the whole project and, inevitably, some parts of the service will be subsidised by other parts requiring fewer resources. Omission of a substantial element could upset the balance of the fee. For instance, it may be decided at the end of work stage D that the production equipment, previously included in the cost of construction, should become a direct contract, without the involvement of the architect.

Where either the percentage fee or the calculated lump sum applies, the basic fee would be adjusted downwards although the architect had provided the necessary services.

WORKED EXAMPLE: OMISSION OF WORK IN THE ORIGINAL BRIEF

Say the original cost of construction was £2.5 million, of which the equipment installation was £0.5 million, and an overall 6 per cent fee applied; the architect might claim a fee as follows:

Fee = 6% of x 40%* x £0.5 million + time charges for removing references from the design information.

** where 40 per cent is used as a multiplying factor to reflect the project percentage completion achieved*

CLIENT VARIATIONS DURING THE CONSTRUCTION PERIOD

When the client requires changes to be made during the construction period, the provisions of the agreement for extra work will apply. Note that where the basic fee is calculated as a percentage fee and inclusion of the variations reduces the cost of construction, the basic fee will be reduced also. However, if the variations increase the cost of construction, in addition to any other fees claimable, the basic fee covering the design and construction stages will also increase.

RESEARCH INTO ADDITIONAL FACILITIES

If the client asks the architect to investigate the provision of an additional facility, for example an additional floor, the research and consequent report will be chargeable under the provisions of the agreement for extra work, whether or not the facilities are included in the final project. If included, the basic fee would be adjusted for the next work stages as noted under 'Revision to brief or client's instructions' above.

SUMMARY

- Fees can be set with reference to empirical data (i.e. from the cost and profit records of similar projects undertaken in the past) or with reference to the time and resources needed to deliver the project. An appropriate profit or contribution margin would then need to be added. A combination of both of these methods is probably the best solution for most architects.
- The RIBA Fees Calculator can be used to build up a fee proposal that will cover costs and give small practices a margin of profit.
- Percentage fees are easy to understand and calculate but may produce a distorted result if there is a significant cost overrun or underspend.
- Lump sum fees have the advantage of giving both parties clarity. However, some room for fee flexibility needs to be built in to the agreement when significant project variations arise.
- Time charge fees are ideal for ad hoc pieces of work where the amount of architect input required is hard to predict at the outset. However, some clients dislike the open cheque-book aspect of this approach.

- Unit price fees may be appropriate where there is a substantial repetition in the work.
- Licences are appropriate if the design work is to be used elsewhere on other projects in which the architect has no further involvement.
- Expenses may be reimbursed in a variety of ways or be included in the overall fee. The architect needs to be aware of the potential erosion of profit that can arise from project expenses.
- Changes inevitably occur on construction projects and the fee agreement should provide a mechanism for dealing with the implications of these changes.

06

FORECASTING FEES

FORECASTING FUTURE FEES

If you have followed the advice set out so far in this book, your practice will be set on a solid financial foundation and you will know where you are and how you got there. Now we are ready to move on to the uncertain world of forecasting the future.

I have always promoted the idea that accounting is much more of an art than a science - indeed the picture of the past that it paints is much more in the style of the Impressionists than the Realists.

Financial statements have a comforting and seductive air of accuracy and authority. Yet those of us who have been involved in their production know that there has been considerable scope for judgement and interpretation in putting the numbers together. This means that the resulting figures are the best approximation of the business situation as it stands. Others may have taken a different view and would have produced an equally 'accurate' yet different set of financial results.

The accountancy bodies have worked for many years to produce a series of standards that would result in financial statements being produced in a consistent way. This quest has been expanded to a global level with the recent development of international accounting standards designed to apply across all borders. Yet the problem remains that businesses are so diverse it is impossible to formulate a single set of rules that will apply and be appropriate in all cases.

Hence, there will always be a need for judgement and differences of opinion and approach.

If arriving at an accurate image of the past is so difficult, how are you to approach the task of working out what the future will hold? The starting point has to be taking a look at the prospects for income represented - in the case of an architecture practice - by a schedule of future fees.

Captive fees

This spreadsheet shows the fees which the practice plans to invoice in the coming six months (although in practice, it could be up to twelve months). This is the best indicator we have of how busy the practice is likely to be in the short to medium term.

excessive optimism when it comes to the subject of fees. I have been lulled into a false sense of security many times on being told that a project has been won and therefore a fee is going to be forthcoming, only to discover that this was not the case. Clients can change their mind at the last moment or simply decide not to go ahead with the project or to delay the start date. From the financial point of view this all amounts to the same end result: no fee is shown on the current captive fee chart.

The example below shows the fees that we expect to be able to invoice on a monthly basis by individual project. These are then added to arrive at a total for each month.

Captive fees forecast

	Fees (£000s)							*Future years*
Project	***Apr***	***May***	***Jun***	***Jul***	***Aug***	***Sept***	***Total***	
Project A	*75*	*75*	*50*	*10*			***210***	*150*
Project B	*50*	*50*	*75*	*100*	*25*	*25*	***325***	*250*
Project C	*25*	*25*		*15*			***65***	
Project D	*10*	*10*	*10*	*10*	*10*	*10*	***60***	
Project E	*75*	*20*	*15*	*20*			***130***	
Total	***235***	***180***	***150***	***155***	***35***	***35***	***790***	***400***

The term 'captive' means that the fees are agreed, fully documented, contractually binding and scheduled for current projects. Only when projects have achieved this degree of certainty are they added to this chart. Prior to achieving this status the projects form part of a mixed bag of 'possible fees' (see page 50).

Experience has taught me that my architect colleagues do suffer from

As the year elapses the forecast figures are replaced with the actual figures achieved, and the balance of the forecast is revised accordingly. It's an interesting exercise to compare the forecast billing in each month with the actual figures achieved to see what differences arose and why.

As noted earlier, the ability to invoice is often delayed by events on the project that are beyond the control of the practice. Consequently, it may be necessary to slide a project's fee profile sideways to the right of the chart, indicating that those invoices will now be raised in later months.

It is a good idea to take steps to stop this 'slippery' process from becoming too much of a habit. If a culture arises in the practice whereby it is considered acceptable or even expected that fee schedules will slip, this can lead to a dangerous short-term cash flow position. It's good practice to promote a culture of fee commitment in which everyone understands that an entry on the captive fee schedule is taken as a promise to deliver that fee for the practice in that particular month. Fee slippage is then viewed in a poor light and discouraged by peer pressure.

As with the majority of financial reports, the captive fee schedule is most easily read from the bottom up.

Monthly expenses and a monthly cash breakeven figure were already developed during the budget process. (The cash breakeven figure is simply the accounting breakeven figure with non-cash items such as depreciation added back.) So it is possible to quickly scan across the months in the total line on the captive fee forecast and see if there may be a problem in meeting the budgeted commitments.

For example, let's assume that the cash breakeven figure in the above example is £180,000. Looking at the chart, April and May appear to be fine, but there is currently a problem in June and July, so we would like to see more fees in those columns to at least bring us up to the £180,000 figure. Beyond that, August and September are currently a long way below what they need to be. If the reality worked out in line with this forecast the practice would soon have a very serious financial problem!

This would typically be visible as a 'cliff edge' profile as shown below.

Cliff edge profile

The cliff edge profile reflects the normal work winning/delivery cycle. Most architects find themselves in the position of being too busy today, reasonably busy for the next few months and then potentially seriously short of work thereafter. The trick is to ensure that this cliff edge does not advance too close.

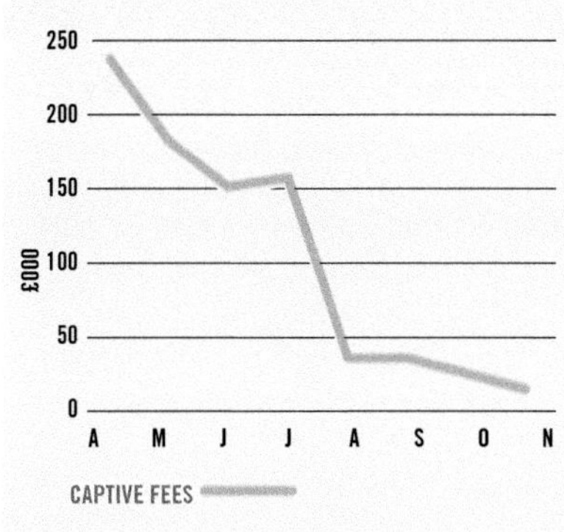

At SEH we have found that all will be well, as long as we can keep our captive fees forecast at breakeven level or above for the coming six months. If the cliff edge does start to become uncomfortably close (e.g. only two or three months away), that is the time for us to devote substantial energy on the sales and marketing fronts, to see if any of the possible jobs that have been incubating for some time can be encouraged to hatch.

Happily, the gloomy scenario predicted six months or so ahead rarely happens.

The comfortable position for the 'cliff edge' will vary from practice to practice, depending on the nature of its work. Practices working on smaller, more short-term 'quick-fire' projects can be comfortable with a cliff edge of say three to six months. For a practice focusing on larger longer-term projects that take longer to secure, such as hospitals or infrastructure projects, a cliff edge closer than twelve months may be a serious cause for concern.

FUTURE POSSIBLE FEES

All of the future fees that the practice hopes to earn and which are anything other than completely certain (i.e. captive) should be classified as 'possibles'. These possibles can often form quite a long list and will include many different projects and potential work situations, ranging from projects that are all but won, but which are just awaiting the final sign off from the client, to a project in which the practice has done no more than express an initial interest.

It is essential to keep a written record of all these opportunities and to track their progress. Hopefully, there will be a constant, gradual conversion process happening, taking projects off the possible list and onto the captive fees list.

The mixed nature of these projects presents the practice with a problem, in accountancy terms, because some are much more likely to become real jobs than others. Therefore it is important to develop a way of quantifying the probability of winning each job and deriving some form of weighted average total that can be compared from month to month.

The possible fees forecast is one way to achieve this.

Possible fees forecast

This spreadsheet estimates the likelihood of future fee levels by taking all of the potential work that is currently being pursued and applying a 'success probability factor' to each project. All of these probabilities and time-adjusted values are then totalled to produce a value that can be

Possible fees forecast

£000

Project	*Project value*	*Fee (%)*	*Fee*	*Probability (%)*	*Probable fee*	*No of years*	*Probable fee per year*
Project A	*£25,000*	*4*	*£1,000*	*25*	*£250*	*2*	*£125*
Project B	*£350*	*7*	*£25*	*75*	*£18*	*1*	*£18*
Project C	*£12,000*	*3*	*£360*	*50*	*£180*	*3*	*£60*
Project D	*£1,500*	*3*	*£45*	*75*	*£34*	*1*	*£34*
Project E	*£52,000*	*4*	*£2,080*	*10*	*£208*	*4*	*£52*
Project F	*£45,000*	*5*	*£2,250*	*5*	*£113*	*4*	*£28*
							£317

WORKED EXAMPLE: POSSIBLE FEES

Potential fee	**£100,000**
Estimated probability of winning	**25%**
Period over which the fee would be earned	**2 years**
Adjusted 'possible' value, per year =	**£100,000 x 25% x 0.5 = £12,500**

compared with the equivalent value that was calculated in the previous months. The aim is to attempt to predict medium-to long-term fees.

The example shown opposite represents a wide variety of projects in terms of both size of fee and likelihood of success. For example, Project A has a 25 per cent probability of success; this could be because the practice is on the final shortlist of four firms. Project B is shown with a 75 per cent probability of success (perhaps this represents a new instruction from an existing client, where there is no other architect involved and hence no competition), but the project still needs budget approval before it can begin. Project F is considered to have just a 5 per cent chance of happening; perhaps this is a project this just at the 'expression of interest' stage.

Furthermore, if these fees were to be won, they would be delivered over different periods of time. Some will happen in the coming year, but others will have fees that are spread over a number of future years. Therefore it is important to have a method that attempts to reconcile these variables and presents an indicative value that can be monitored from month to month, to see if a trend is emerging.

The simplest way to do this, is to derive an adjusted value for each project by taking the fee value, applying a probability factor, then annualising it by dividing by the number of years that the project would run, as shown above.

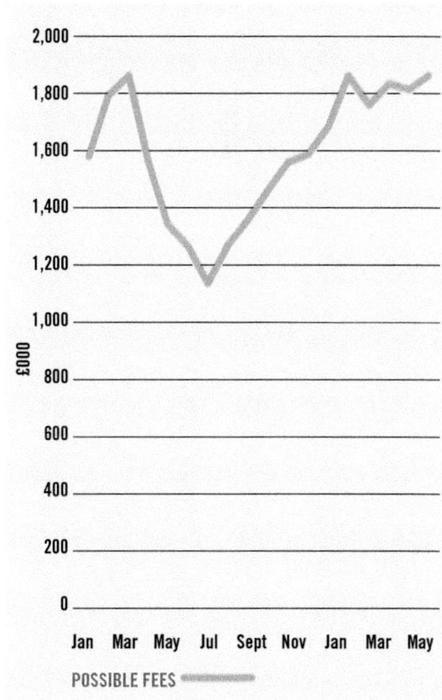

The same calculation is performed for each potential project and a total figure is derived. In itself this total figure has no great meaning. Ultimately a potential fee is either won or it is not. However, when it is tracked over a number of months it can be a useful predictor of future fee levels with resulting charges shown in the graph on the proceeding page.

Each practice should develop its own model to suit its own particular needs. What is important is that some attempt is made to predict the future levels of fees that will result from all of the current marketing activity.

The method described above is just one possible suggested solution, which I have found useful in our practice. We have been working with this particular method of evaluating possible fees for many years now and have found it to be a reasonably reliable predictor of future captive fees. There does seem to be a measurable nine- to twelve-month correlated lag between an increase or decrease in the total 'possible' figure and a similar effect mirrored in the actual fees achieved.

The possible fees chart can be strangely cruel. Imagine that you just won a major new project which you had been pursuing for some time. The successful team involved in the bid are rightly congratulated and the celebratory champagne is duly sipped; the design team is assembled and work duly begins. But when, a few days later, you revisit the updated possible fees chart you discover, somewhat to your dismay, that it has now suddenly plunged downwards.

The winning of the job means that it has become a 'captive' fee and therefore it has disappeared from the possibles list and the overall total. This serves as a reminder of the harsh reality of the situation: it is great to have won the work, but now you need to begin again, to win the work needed to keep the business going for the next twelve months.

A COMBINED FEE FORECAST

Smaller practices may find it helpful to prepare a combined fees forecast, as shown opposite.

Combined fees forecast
This shows the overall picture for both captive and possible fees on a month by month basis. It is of course important to continue to appreciate the distinction between those types of fees shown in the top of the chart which are already contractually agreed, and those in the bottom half which you can only hope will happen.

In this example the overall monthly total seems to be reasonably consistent throughout the period of the forecast. However, in the latter months (August and September) the forecasts are still heavily dependent on fees that are yet to be confirmed and therefore it is important to try to convert these into captive fees as soon as possible.

Combining these two fee forecasts can a good indication of how busy the practice is going to be in the short and medium term. It is easy to see whether more resources will be needed to do the work on hand, or perhaps that the marketing drive needs to increase to ensure a flow of new work in the future.

Fee forecast chart								
Captive fees	***Apr***	***May***	***Jun***	***Jul***	***Aug***	***Sep***	***TOTAL***	***Future years***
Project A	*75*	*75*	*50*	*10*			*210*	*150*
Project B	*50*	*50*	*75*	*100*	*25*	*25*	*325*	*200*
Project C	*25*	*25*		*15*			*65*	
Project D	*10*	*10*	*10*	*10*	*10*	*10*	*60*	
Project E	*75*	*20*	*15*	*20*			*130*	
Total captive fees	***235***	***180***	***150***	***155***	***35***	***35***	***790***	***400***
Possible fees								
Project X	*15*	*15*	*10*				*40*	
Project Y	*20*	*25*	*25*	*15*	*45*	*45*	*175*	*125*
Project X				*25*	*75*	*90*	*190*	*75*
Total possible fees	***35***	***40***	***35***	***40***	***12***	***135***	***405***	***200***
Combined total fees	***270***	***220***	***185***	***195***	***155***	***170***	***1195***	***600***

THE RESOURCES FORECAST

The captive fees forecast described above shows how much work is on hand and indicates how full the order book is for the next three to six months. This information can then be linked through directly to the cash inflow section of the cash flow forecast (Chapter 7), to illustrate the solvency position over the next nine to twelve months.

Next you need to know whether the practice has the right number of people available to be able to deliver the work lined up in the captive fees forecast. A resources forecast will provide this information.

Resources forecast

This is a rolling, weekly forecast of the people that will be needed on a project by project basis, compared with the total number of people available.

Project resource forecast							
Number of people required			***May***				***June***
Week ending	*3*	*10*	*17*	*24*	*31*	*7*	*14*
Project A	*4*	*4*	*4*	*4*	*3*	*3*	*2*
Project B	*2.5*	*3*	*3*	*1*	*1.5*	*0*	*0*
Project C	*3.5*	*3.5*	*3.5*	*4*	*2*	*2*	*1*
Project D	*2*	*2*	*2*	*1*	*3*	*3*	*3*
People required	*12*	*12.5*	*12.5*	*10*	*9.5*	*8*	*6*
People available	*14*	*14*	*12*	*12*	*12*	*10*	*10*
Net position (surplus/shortage)	***2***	***1.5***	***-0.5***	***2***	***2.5***	***2***	***4***

This forecast spreadsheet shows immediately where shortages or surpluses may occur. Like the captive fees forecast, it needs to be updated regularly (e.g. weekly) to accurately reflect the way that the resourcing needs of projects tend to fluctuate as the work progresses. These are not only project-related changes, but people changes too – to take account of holidays, study leave, sickness and so on. These factors are deducted in order to arrive at the 'people available' figure.

Someone in the practice needs to make a commitment to invest the time in keeping the details up to date, but in my experience this effort is well rewarded because it gives you the ability to see resource problems coming two or three months ahead. This is generally early enough to solve the problem before it becomes a crisis.

It is also important to plan for some flexibility so that there are always some resources available to help with the general marketing effort such as submissions for new work, working on design competitions or perhaps updating the practice's website or promotional material.

This can be very hard to achieve, especially when there is great pressure on teams to deliver against a deadline. But it is just another aspect of the constant need to keep winning new work for the future to ensure that the practice survives. The forecast may show that two people are allocated to 'marketing'. However, what this usually means is that ten people will each be spending some part of their time on these activities over the course of the week, blended in with their other project activities. When all of these pieces of individual marketing activity are aggregated they will amount to the equivalent of two people working full time on the marketing front.

A graphical view of the resources data will tend to echo the shape of the captive fees graph. But whereas the captive fees has a cliff edge some six to nine months away, the resources chart will have the reverse of this – a 'cliff face' that also appears in about six to nine months' time, when it seems as if there will be a lot of people free with no project work to do.

Resources cliff face

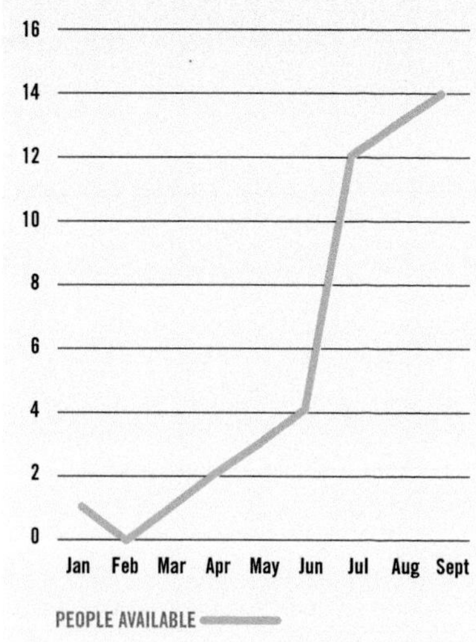

Like all of the charts described in this book, the resources charts are most useful when showing trends over time. The resources chart tends to follow a familiar pattern. There always seems to be more work to do right now than we have the people to do it. The weekly column may well show a net position of –2 or –3, which means that the practice could really do with a couple of extra people now and next week.

However, it does seem that things will calm down shortly and that balance will be restored – the chart shows 0. So everyone will have to get their heads down (again) for the next week or so to meet the deadlines, comforted by the knowledge that it will get easier soon as the cavalry arrives in the form of people becoming free from their other current project commitments – the chart starts to show +2 or +3. Then we hit the cliff face in about six months' time where it looks as if over half of the practice will be sitting around drinking coffee and reading magazines waiting for the phone to ring.

In reality this tends to be a fairly constant position. As new smaller pieces of work filter in or current projects expand or change, there is always more to do than we had anticipated. So at SEH, when we see a consistent number of weeks with a –2 or –4 ahead we know that it is time to look for some extra people – either by recruitment or by arranging to get in some temporary resources to meet some specific project deadlines.

The process begins with the chart below, which shows who will be working on each project over the next few weeks. The resulting net available figures are then linked through to the overall resources chart.

In my experience, projects rarely run to their expected timetable. They can quite suddenly accelerate when a client brings a deadline forward, or be temporarily frozen, perhaps when an unexpected delay occurs in gaining a planning consent, or funding is not becoming available when expected. Each of these events causes a rapid shift in the resources balance and the need for some swift revisions to the plan.

Overlaid on this is the desire to meet the aspirations of the individual architect or team member.

Allocation of staff resources

People allocation forecast							
			May				*June*
Week ending	***3***	***10***	***17***	***24***	***31***	***7***	***14***
Name							
N Foster		*proj A*		*holiday*		*proj A*	
R Rogers		*proj B*				*marketing*	*marketing*
Z Hadid	*study*			*proj C*			
F L Wright		*proj A*				*proj C*	
I Brunel						*holiday*	*leaver*
Total available for project work	***4***	***5***	***5***	***4***	***4***	***3***	***3***
Study	*1*	*0*	*0*	*0*	*0*	*0*	*0*
Holiday	*0*	*0*	*0*	*1*	*0*	*1*	*0*
Marketing	*0*	*0*	*0*	*0*	*1*	*1*	*1*
Total people	***5***	***5***	***5***	***5***	***5***	***5***	***4***

Understandably, the individual wants the stimulation of new challenges and to gain experience of working on a variety of building types across a range of sectors. Yet from the practice's point of view the most efficient way to resource a project is to use people who have recent experience of working on a similar sort of project and who have gained expertise that will allow them to achieve a good result swiftly.

The need to manage this potential conflict successfully makes the resource planning process critical to the success of the practice. It requires a detailed knowledge of how projects work, complemented by sensitivity to the needs and desires of the individuals involved, and combined with an eye to how a particular group of people will function as a team.

Frustratingly, once this elusive balance is achieved, the chances are that something will come along to upset it in a matter of days, so that the whole plan will need to be re-addressed so that a new balance can be reached.

The allocation of people to projects is always going to be one of the most challenging tasks that the management of an architectural practice will face.

SUMMARY

- Fees are either firm/captive (i.e. covered by a contractual agreement and are, as far as anyone can predict, definitely going to happen at a predictable time) or possible (with various levels of certainty).
- Captive fees tend to be predictable for the next three or six months, but beyond that they fall off the edge of the cliff. The constant mission of the practice is to ensure that this cliff edge does not come too close, but is kept at a constant distance in the future.
- Possible fees can be compared from month to month by applying a simple calculation to give a single indicator.
- By monitoring captive and possible fees you can obtain a good sense of the short- and medium-term prospects for work that can be invoiced.
- These charts need to be constantly updated as events change, if they are to retain their relevance and usefulness.
- Projects are often delayed or rescheduled and this will have a knock-on effect on fee billing, which needs to be kept under constant review.
- It is essential to develop a resource plan, as a way to predict whether there are people with the right level of skills available to deliver the work.
- Resources planning needs to take account of all the other essential but non-fee-earning tasks, especially marketing.
- Resources planning also needs to take account of the professional aspirations of the individual architect.
- Resources planning is the most difficult part of the whole process of financial forecasting, but it is crucial because so much money is invested in people.

CASH FLOW MANAGEMENT

All accountants and bank managers (although I should probably use their preferred title of 'relationship managers' these days) love cash flow forecasts. The reason they like them so much is that they know cash flow forecasts are the most accurate way to predict the future financial health of the business, both in the short and medium term. Accountants know, from their experience in dealing with insolvency, that most businesses fail when they simply run out of cash. The popular misconception is that businesses are forced to close because they failed to make a profit or to find sufficient customers. The truth is that the majority are forced into liquidation because they could no longer meet their financial obligations when they fell due and the bank's goodwill had been exhausted.

CASH FLOW FORECAST – A DEFINITION

The cash flow forecast is a rolling statement of all of the cash inflows and outflows for the practice which predicts the month end cash balance for a number of months ahead. This is one of the most important reports for an architect to monitor in order to get a view of when a cash shortage problem may be approaching.

You will commonly hear the directors of a recently declared insolvent company make comments such as: 'If only that major customer had paid us on time then we would have survived'. I often refer to the quarterly VAT payment as the 'dreaded VAT payment' – which gets that name because it is often the final straw. It is the last large payment that simply cannot be met, and which pushes the business that has been teetering on the brink of its overdraft limit for the last few months over the edge. As a number of professional football clubs have discovered in recent years it is often the VAT department of HMRC that initiates winding-up procedures.

The cash flow forecast is one of the key documents that the bank will want to see regularly in support of its overdraft facilities, and it is important to ensure that it is as accurate as possible. The bank will look back and review the accuracy of the cash flow forecasts that they have been given in the past. They understand that these were forecasts and will not expect them to be entirely accurate. However, if they can see that the forecasts are consistently very inaccurate, they will begin to have doubts about the competence of the management team, and the practice's ability to manage its own financial affairs.

If the bank feels uncomfortable, it may be unwilling to renew the overdraft facility when it falls due, which could have serious financial consequences. It is worth remembering that bank overdrafts are repayable on demand, which means that the bank does have a right to ask the practice for the entire amount outstanding on the overdraft to be paid back within a few days.

The chart opposite shows a typical cash flow forecast.

The cash flow forecast is the most important tool available for predicting the continuing financial health of the practice. Like many financial reports, it is most easily read from the bottom up. The row at the foot of the page shows the predicted final (closing) bank balance the end of each month. This shows at a glance if there is going to be a cash flow problem and when it is likely to arise.

In common with the captive and possible fees and resources spreadsheets, the cash flow forecast is a rolling forecast – in the example above, it is a rolling six-month forecast. This means that the forecast is revised each month and in so doing the first month is removed and a new month is added on the end.

Each practice will have to establish a suitable forecast period to suit its needs. For smaller practices it is like to be up to 6 months, whereas larger practices may well be able to work meaningfully with a 12 or 18 month forecast.

Cash flow forecast							
INFLOWS (£000s)	***May***	***June***	***July***	***Aug***	***Sept***	***Oct***	***Totals (£000s)***
Opening balance	*-£32*	*£87.6*	*£45.4*	*£55.4*	*£39.4*	*-£59.6*	
Fees collected (60 days)	*£250*	*£145*	*£175*	*£155*	*£165*	*£225*	
VAT collected	*£12*	*£15*	*£18*	*£16*	*£18*	*£20*	
Total cash INFLOWS	*£262*	*£160*	*£193*	*£171*	*£183*	*£245*	***£1,214***
OUTFLOWS (£000s)	***May***	***June***	***July***	***Aug***	***Sept***	***Oct***	***Totals (£000s)***
Net payroll	*£66*	*£68*	*£70*	*£75*	*£75*	*£75*	
PAYE and NI	*£26.4*	*£27.2*	*£28*	*£30*	*£30*	*£30*	
Rent and service charge	*£12*	*£12*	*£15*	*£12*	*£12*	*£15*	
PII	*£0*	*£7*	*£7*	*£7*	*£7*	*£7*	
Sub-consultant payments	*£5*	*£5*	*£5*	*£5*	*£5*	*£5*	
Supplier payments	*£30*	*£30*	*£30*	*£30*	*£30*	*£30*	
Input VAT	*£3*	*£3*	*£3*	*£3*	*£3*	*£3*	
VAT payment	*£0*	*£50*	*£0*	*£0*	*£45*	*£0*	
Corporation tax	*£0*	*£0*	*£0*	*£0*	*£50*	*£0*	
Capital expenditure	*£0*	*£0*	*£25*	*£25*	*£25*	*£25*	
Total cash OUTFLOWS	***£142.4***	***£202.2***	***£183***	***£187***	***£282***	***£190***	***£1,186.6***
	May	***June***	***July***	***Aug***	***Sept***	***Oct***	
Closing balance	***£87.6***	***£45.4***	***£55.4***	***£39.4***	***-£59.6***	***-£4.6***	

Cash flow forecast
This is the classic report prepared by finance people all over the world and the bank manager's favourite. It shows the amount of money that is predicted to flow in and out of the practice and the projected bank balance at the end of each month.

USING LONGER-TERM CASH FLOW FORECASTS TO ASSESS THE BUSINESS VIABILITY

The example cash flow forecast shown above is a model based on normal operating conditions. If the practice is considering approaching the bank about financing a major new project (such as the purchase of new premises or the acquisition of another practice) it will need to produce cash flow forecast extended up to two or even three years in support of the application.

In addition, for end-of-year accounting purposes accountants and auditors may require some long-term cash flow forecasts to support a 'going concern' assumption for the business. Once the practice is large enough to require a formal audit, the accountants will need to produce accounts to which they are prepared to sign a declaration that the accounts that they have prepared show a 'true and fair view' of the financial position of the business. As a part of this process the accountants will take a view on the ability of the business to keep operating in its current form and the long-term cash flow forecast will be a key report that will enable them to do this.

It is interesting to check the total value of inflows against the total value of outflows over the course of the forecast period to get a sense of overall liquidity.

In the example, total inflows for the six months are £1.214 million, whereas total outflows are expected to be £1.187 million, indicating a potentially balanced position across the period. As this forecast is directly linked to the fee forecast described in Chapter 6 it will tend to follow a similar pattern. Most cash flow forecasts show an improving position over the next quarter or two, and then a rapid deterioration six months or so later. This reflects the uncertainty of future fees and the financial 'cliff edge' effect that all practices tend to face in the medium term.

Cash flow is often described as the lifeblood of the business. It is useful to think of cash in these terms: something that needs to keep circulating in order to keep each part of the practice healthy.

Equally - although it is not usually a problem that many architecture practices have - it is also not a good idea to sit on a large cash pile for too long. Money needs to flow and to be used creatively, rather than just be left to accumulate in the bank account. This is especially true in the current ultra-low interest rate environment.

It is worth looking at this forecast in some detail.

CASH INFLOWS

The top section of the cash flow chart shows the money that is coming into the practice, of which the largest element is the collection of fees from clients. For this you need to make an honest and realistic assumption about how quickly the fees are being paid. Most practices will have standard

WORKED EXAMPLE: CALCULATING 'DEBTOR DAYS'

$$\text{Average 'debtor days'} = \frac{\text{Average amount due from clients at month end} \times 365}{\text{Annual gross fees income}}$$

For example, say the annual gross fee income (including VAT) is £200,000, and the average amount due from clients at the month end is £33,000:

$$\text{Average 'debtor days'} = \frac{£33{,}000 \times 365}{£200{,}000} = \text{60 days (approximately)}$$

This means that on average it takes 60 days to collect the fees that are invoiced.

Equally, you can perform a similar calculation for 'creditor days' (i.e. how long does it take on average to pay your suppliers).

$$\text{Average 'creditor days'} = \frac{\text{Average amount due to suppliers (creditors) at month end} \times 365}{\text{Annual gross cost of overheads (from the budget)}}$$

If the average amount due is £15,000 and the annual gross cost of overheads is £100,000, then

$$\text{Average 'creditor days'} = \frac{£15{,}000 \times 365}{£100{,}000} = \text{55 creditor days (approx)}$$

payment terms of 30 days, but that does not mean this will actually be achieved. Therefore, you need to work with the reality of the situation based on experience, which you can do by calculation of the average 'debtor days' as shown above.

These examples represent a balanced scenario, in which the practice is being paid at a broadly similar rate to the speed with which it is settling the bills with suppliers. At SEH, we set target debtor and creditor days as a part of our annual budget process and monitor the ongoing trends on a monthly basis as part of our KPI package.

These calculations become the working assumptions to be used for cash flow purposes.

Using these values, you can fill in the fees collected row in the cash flow spreadsheet by taking the figures from the captive fees forecast and entering them into the anticipated cash flow two months later. This means that fees invoiced in January are assumed to be collected in March, and so on.

It is good practice for the cash flow forecast to show the key assumptions as a footnote, so that anyone looking at it can make a judgement about the reasonableness of the assumptions and thus the reliability of the cash flow built on those assumptions.

ACCOUNTING FOR VAT

The cash flow forecast needs to account for all the money going in and out of the practice, so it must allow for the effects of VAT.

Assuming that your clients are all UK-based and VAT registered, you will need to add 20 per cent to the fees collected as an inflow of cash. You also need to estimate how much VAT you pay to your suppliers and enter that figure as a cash outflow. Then you need to plan to pay HMRC the net VAT, usually on a quarterly basis (where net VAT is simply the VAT you have collected from customers minus the VAT you have paid out to suppliers in the most recent three-month reporting period, i.e. net VAT = output VAT - input VAT). It is important to be prepared for this relatively large payment.

While on the subject of VAT, it is worth mentioning the potential attractions of HMRC's Flat Rate Scheme (FRS). This can work well for professional service firms such as architects where all, or the vast majority, of the work is for UK-based VAT registered clients, and the practice does not incur a large amount of input VAT (i.e. payments of VAT to its own suppliers). The FRS is attractive because it is much simpler to administer than the normal quarterly accounting for all income and expenses, and can also result in a small 'profit' for the practice. At the time of writing, the FRS percentage applicable to architects is 14.5 per cent. It is worth exploring with your accountant whether the FRS would work well in your particular circumstances.

WORKED EXAMPLE: FRS CALCULATION

Value of sales invoiced in the three-month period	**£100,000**
VAT added to sales (at 20%)	**£20,000**
Total	**£120,000**
Apply the FRS percentage to the total:	
14.5% of £120,000 =	**£17,400**

That is the figure to be paid across to HMRC.

Note that the practice has, of course, collected £20,000 of output VAT from its clients, and has therefore made a gain of £2,600.

In this simplified method no input tax is claimed, so this 'gain' is the allowance for the VAT that has been paid to suppliers in the period but not claimed.

There is even an additional first year incentive whereby the rate used is reduced by 1 per cent - which gives the small business an even greater 'profit'.

CASH OUTFLOWS

The first thing that you will notice on the cash flow forecast spreadsheet above is that there are many more rows in the outflows section than there are in the inflow sections. As with the rest of our lives, there always seem to be many more ways to spend money than there are ways to earn it!

Even in the simple example forecast there are a number of lines which represent groups of expenses. It is essential to ensure that all of the many types of practice expenditure are included somewhere in the cash flow, perhaps by working through the detailed Profit and Loss account on a line by line basis. It could also be useful to pore over old bank statements to look for items that have been missed or which only arise occasionally (e.g. annual subscriptions or insurance renewals). I like to keep a rolling comparison of my monthly cash flow forecast with the actual cash flow achieved. This is a good feedback mechanism that can help to improve the accuracy of the cash flow forecast process for the future.

The largest single regular cash outflow is likely to be the payroll. The associated PAYE income tax and NI contributions are deducted from salaries and have to be paid across to HMRC by the middle of the following month. The total payroll figure for any given month is split over two months, with the net pay (i.e. after tax deductions) going out in the first month and the PAYE and NI deductions relating to it being paid to HMRC in the following month. In the normal course of events this makes little difference, because the total outflows are much the same from month to month. However, it's important to model the effects of the annual pay review and the payment of any irregular bonuses.

It is important to identify separately all significant single items of expenditure, such as the PII premium, which may have to be paid in a single instalment or perhaps be spread over a number of months (as it is in the example above).

It also helpful to identify the payments that need to be made to the members of the design team for which the architect is acting as lead consultant for invoicing and payment purposes. These can be significant amounts and can have a serious impact on the overall cash flow position, especially if the architect has to pay the consultant before having collected the equivalent funds from the client. This can represent a significant risk for which the architect receives little if any reward.

Finally, you need to ensure that you include those items of capital expenditure that were identified in the capital budget. This can require large sums to be spent at a particular point in time. The cash flow forecast may suggest that you should consider entering into suitable finance arrangements (e.g. leasing for the purchase of computer equipment) if outright purchase would seem to be straining the cash flow unduly.

ACCOUNTING FOR TAXATION

The payment of income tax and corporation tax are the other significant items to be included in the list of cash outflows. For partnerships or LLPs there will be self-assessment income tax payments to be made in January and July of each year. For companies, there will be a single annual corporation tax payment, of approximately 20 per cent of profits, to be made to HMRC within nine months and a day of the end of the company's financial year.

SUMMARY

- Cash is the lifeblood of any business. It represents the flow of energy through the body of the practice. It needs to be kept moving and it needs to be constantly refreshed.
- The cash flow forecast is one the most important financial control reports.
- If the bank has provided finance in the form of an overdraft or loan it will certainly expect to see the cash flow forecast at regular intervals.
- Periodic payments such as income tax and VAT are often the straw that breaks the camel's back. The practice may be just managing to keep its head above water from month to month in financial terms when a large tax bill comes along which simply cannot be paid.
- As well as the day-to-day income and expenses, cash flow forecasts need to take account of other items such as capital expenditure on cars, computer equipment and furniture, which can require large amounts of cash to be found at a particular point in the year and can throw the whole cash flow plan adrift.

CREDIT CONTROL

Having gone to all the trouble of winning the project, seeing the work through to the client's satisfaction and sending in the final fee invoice, it is hard to understand why any architect or practice would then neglect to ask for their bill to be paid. Yet it is surprising how often this seems to happen. The professional time and effort to which the invoice relates probably took place a number of months before, so why should you accept any further delay at the payment stage?

Good organisation is the key to effective credit control. The collection process does not need to be either aggressive or apologetic; it just needs to be performed in a regular and determined way until the desired result is achieved.

There is still some reluctance among architects and many other professionals to talk to their clients about outstanding fees. There can be a feeling that this sort of conversation will in some way damage the relationship with the client. In fact, I have found the opposite to be true. Clients do not respect architects who do not run their own financial affairs in a business-like way. Indeed, they may wonder how professionally and efficiently the architect is dealing with their own project and money if they do not seem concerned about running their own practice professionally.

Ideally, the credit control process should begin before any design work has been done at all. Unless the client is known to you from a previous project or has been referred from a trusted source, it's wise to undertake some form of credit checking to see if they have a good record of keeping their payment promises. There are several companies and organisations that provide reports that give an objective view of a potential client's creditworthiness, based on the experience of others. It's not just a question of whether the potential client pays or not, it is also a matter of how quickly they pay and to what extent they observe other people's payment terms. It could make a significant difference to the firm's cash flow if a major client routinely takes an average of 60 days to pay rather than the agreed 30 days.

As soon as you start to work for a client and allow professional time to be devoted to that client's project, you are effectively extending them credit. You would not dream of loaning money from the practice's bank account to someone without first checking to see if they are able or likely to repay you. The same principle should apply in this situation which in fact is exactly the same.

Once it has been established that the client is creditworthy, the credit control process begins with the negotiation of contract terms. Most payment problems stem from an initial misunderstanding between the architect and client. These misunderstandings arise from uncertainty in one or all of these areas:

- The exact scope of the work to be done
- The precise terms of the contract
- The amount and timing of the fees to be paid
- The method to be used for the calculation of the fees.

Most clients will only deliberately withhold payment of an architect's invoice as a last resort. This is a dramatic gesture and signals the fact that earlier warning signs have been ignored. This tends to occur at a fairly late stage in the deterioration of the relationship with the client, when emotions may well be running high. Yet at the heart of the problem will be a difference in expectation that has not been addressed, either in the original agreement or in subsequent meetings or communications.

One of the many advantages of using the RIBA standard forms of agreement is that these fundamental terms of payment are already written in. The client may not have read them very closely at the outset, but this provides no defence later if a dispute arises.

It is best practice to keep all of the documentation and emails that relate to fees together in a separate file. This will ensure that it is straightforward to follow the financial progress of the project, and will make it easier to raise invoices (which will often take a set format) and work to a pre-agreed timetable. It will also make it easier to deal with any fee-related questions or disputes that may arise.

LATE PAYMENT

It is also best practice to include a note on the face of each of your invoices to clients reminding them of the agreed payment terms. For example:

Invoices are due upon presentation and payable within 30 days of the invoice date. We reserve the right to charge interest as provided for in our agreement or interest and compensation at the statutory rate on amounts that are not received on time.

This wording makes reference to the legal right to charge interest and claim compensation for the extra administration involved in so doing. These provisions are contained in the Late Payment of Commercial Debts (Interest) Act 1998 as amended and supplemented by the Late Payment of Commercial Debts Regulations 2002. The Act allows for a punitive rate of interest of 8 per cent (which is an extremely high rate of interest given the long-standing 0.5 per cent base rate that has prevailed in the 2010s).

There is also provision for compensation to be paid to cover the administrative costs of having to calculate and charge the interest penalty. The base rates to be used in the calculation are set for six-monthly periods from 1 January to 30 June, and 1 July to 31 December, and are known as the 'reference rate'. The correct rate to be used at any particular time can be found by visiting www.payontime.co.uk, which also includes a helpful interest calculator.

www.payontime.co.uk

WORKED EXAMPLE: CALCULATION OF LATE PAYMENT INTEREST

Let's assume that the current reference rate is 0.5 per cent, making the applicable chargeable interest rate 8.5 per cent. The outstanding debt is for £10,000 and is now 30 days overdue. Note that this is days 'overdue' rather than the number of days outstanding.

The calculation is as follows:

Interest on total = £10,000 x 8.5% = £850

Interest per day = £850/365 = £2.33

Total interest payable to date = interest per day x number of days overdue

= £2.33 x 30 days = £69.90

In addition, at the time of writing, £100 can be added to this interest charge as compensation for the additional administration now involved in the collection of the amount due.

The potential cost of the combination of the two elements (i.e. £69.90 interest plus a £100 admin charge) is a strong incentive to the client to ensure that payment is made on time.

At SEH we have often found that just threatening to make an interest charge is enough for a client to suddenly find that they are able to process one or invoices for payment quickly after all. It is going to give someone in the client's organisation a serious problem to justify to their seniors the reason for having to make payment of an interest and admin invoice that they have received, and it is normally easier and less painful to simply arrange for the invoice to be paid.

The original agreement with the client may have stipulated the terms and conditions under which interest can be charged for late payment. Where an alternative agreement exists, this replaces the provisions of the Act as described above.

Regardless of the approach adopted, there is no reason for the architect to finance the client's business by accepting late payment without some form of compensation.

Some organisations who have their own cash flow problems consciously adopt a policy of only paying suppliers if and when they have been chased. This really is a case of if you do not ask, you will not get!

THE AGED DEBTOR REPORT

The routine collection process begins with the production of an 'aged debtor report', as shown below.

Aged debtor report

This is the credit controller's favourite report. It shows who owes money to the practice and – crucially – for how long it has been outstanding.

Aged debtor report as at [date]						
£	***Current month***	***30–60 days***	***60–90 days***	***90–120 days***	***>120 days***	***Total (£)***
Client A						
Project 1		*£29,375*				
Project 2			*£5,875*			
Project 3	*£11,750*			*£17,625*		
Client B						
Project 4		*£64,625*				
Project 5	*£23,500*			*-£1,175*	*£1,175*	
Client C						
Project 6					*£8,225*	
Project 7		*£7,050*				
Client D						
Project 8				*£47,000*		
Project 9					*£41,125*	
Total	***£35,250***	***£101,050***	***£5,875***	***£63,450***	***£50,525***	***£256,150***
% of total	*14%*	*39%*	*2%*	*25%*	*20%*	

Contrary to the opinion of some of my creative colleagues, this is not about the amounts of money owed to us by wizened old men with long white beards. It's actually about how long each particular sales invoice has been outstanding. Most practices will set collection targets in percentage terms, for example, to ensure that 75 per cent of the total amount owed is received within 30 to 45 days.

All good accounting software packages will include an aged debtor report as one of the standard reports.

This is where a standardised system of credit control comes into its own. Outstanding invoices should be chased soon after they have passed their expected payment date. At this first stage a reminder email with a copy of the outstanding invoice attached is probably sufficient. If a further week or two elapses without receipt of payment, this should be followed up with a phone call. It could well be that the original invoice or follow-up email has failed to reach the correct person and this is the quickest way to get to the source of the problem.

As with all aspects of client management it is important to build a relationship and establish rapport. Delays in payment are often of an administrative nature, especially in large organisations. By building a working relationship with the person dealing with the payment in the client organisation, you can begin to understand their payment systems and work with them accordingly. Many businesses have a system of paying their suppliers on a monthly payment 'run'. By knowing when this takes place during the month (and it is not always at the end of the month), and by sending in your invoices at the correct time, you can ensure that your invoice gets onto the first available payment 'run' and you will receive the money a month earlier than you might have otherwise.

These days it seems to be an increasingly common practice to send out invoices only as attachments to emails. Although this is quick and easy, I still think it is best practice for this to be backed up by the sending of a paper invoice as well. It is much easier to ignore or delete an email and its attachment than it is to ignore a piece of paper. This will arrive on someone's desk and will be a problem to them until such time as they can pass it on or deal with it.

Architects' invoices may need to be approved by a number of different people, both within and outside the client organisation, and this introduces a number of opportunities for the invoice to get 'stuck'. In our practice we deal with many public sector clients and their payment systems will usually require an approved purchase order (PO) number to be quoted before any payments are released. These POs are often quite difficult to get hold of, and it is hard to resist getting on with the design job on hand while waiting for this essential piece of administration to fall into place. But it is important to appreciate that if you spend your professional time on a project that the client has not formally approved you are working at a considerable risk.

If the invoice remains unpaid, you can call on the help of your friendly contact in the client's payments department to chase your invoice through their system. It is surprising how many invoices can get lost in the process, and it may be easier to email copies rather than wait for the originals to be tracked down. Although this duplication introduces the possibility of the accidental payment of the same invoice twice, this rarely seems to happen in practice.

There is often a sort of camaraderie between those who work in the accounts departments of different organisations. Many of them perform the dual role of chasing customer payments, while at the same time being chased themselves for payment by their own suppliers. This shared experience means that there is some sympathy for the opposite number who is chasing for payment and an understanding that it is simply a thankless task that has to be done. Wise credit controllers will work with this mutual understanding to help ensure that the fees of their own practices are paid smoothly and in good time.

The credit control process should result in a gradual and well-documented audit trail.

By the time an invoice has become seriously overdue, say three months, there should be a file showing that there have been regular reminders and requests for payment that have been delivered in a number of different ways (i.e. email, phone calls, letters etc.) throughout this period. Should the matter eventually need to be resolved through a more formal process, as described below, then this file will act as an invaluable source of evidence to show that all reasonable steps have already been taken to encourage the client to pay.

THE 'DROP-THROUGH' AND THE 'MULTIPLIER EFFECT' OF BAD DEBT

As a part of the end of the financial year accounting process, the business has to take a view about how likely it is to collect the amounts shown as outstanding on the aged debtors list. From an accounting point of view, the year-end debtor's balance is a form of asset and it is important to ensure that this asset is not overstated. Amounts where it is unsure whether they will be paid are treated as potential bad debts and you need to reserve against them accordingly. This has the same financial effect as incurring an actual bad debt. The full amount that is written off is deducted as if it were an expense, and in that sense it 'drops through' the Profit and Loss account straight to the bottom line and reduces the net profit accordingly.

It may seem that an unpaid invoice of £10,000 is relatively insignificant to a practice with a £1 million turnover, because it only represents 1 per cent of the overall income. Yet if this practice averages a 10 per cent profit before tax (i.e. £100,000), then this bad debt adjustment of £10,000 now results in a 10 per cent reduction in pre-tax profit.

To look at this another way, the £10,000 bad debt is equivalent to the profit that is earned on £100,000 of turnover. This is known as the 'multiplier effect'. In order to replace the profit lost by failing to collect this debt, the practice will need to generate another £100,000 of work in order to put itself back into the same financial position. When viewed in this context it is easy to see how important it is to pursue all of the amounts that are due, no matter how small. If the work has been done, it is surely only fair to receive payment for it. By failing to collect all that is due you may be reducing your profits by 20 per cent or more per year.

RESOLVING PROBLEMS WITH FEES

When it eventually becomes clear that the issue of an unpaid fee is not going to be resolved by discussion and negotiation between the architect and client, there are a number of more formal ways to resolve the problem. The RIBA offers a number of services to assist with these processes and full details can be found in the 'Professional Support' section of the website www.architecture.com.

www.architecture.com

The RIBA has also developed two new dispute resolution schemes that are offered as alternatives to more formal dispute resolution processes - RIBA Third Party Opinion and RIBA Fixed-Fee Mediation.

Both are designed as low-cost, short-timescale schemes aimed at resolving the sort of low-level impasse that should not delay or derail the project, but all too often does.

The Third Party Opinion sees an independent professional appointed on behalf of the parties to provide a professional opinion and recommendation for a settlement.

The Fixed-Fee Mediation scheme is typically suited to disputes that are of relatively low value, where the parties can reasonably expect the matter to be resolved in a relatively short timescale, and where there is a mutual and genuine wish to settle.

MEDIATION

Mediation is an alternative to adjudication, arbitration and litigation. It is an informal process and does not impose a resolution to the dispute and only becomes binding with the consent of all parties. Mediation allows the parties the freedom to explore ways of settling a dispute with the assistance of an impartial and independent person (the mediator). It is essentially a process in which the mediator assists in negotiations between the parties to arrive at the settlement.

The overall intention of mediation is to reach an agreed solution. If that proves to be impossible then the mediator will attempt to narrow the issues and, if requested to do so by the parties, will make a recommendation as to how the dispute could be settled, but the recommendation is in no way binding unless the parties push it to be so.

The proceedings conducted are privileged and are conducted on a 'without prejudice' basis. This means that nothing disclosed during the mediation process can be used as evidence in any subsequent proceedings.

The RIBA can nominate a mediator from their list of approved professionals.

ADJUDICATION

The Housing Grants, Construction and Regeneration Act of 1996 gives a statutory right to the architect to have disputes resolved by adjudication. The only exception is when one of the parties is the residential occupier of the relevant property.

Adjudication has the benefit of being relatively quick and inexpensive. Without mutual agreement, the issues to be considered and timescales in making decision are prescribed. The decision is binding and the courts will normally enforce the decision promptly if needed. However, either party may raise the issue again in arbitration or litigation or even a related adjudication, for example if the client responds with a counterclaim of negligence.

The RIBA's dispute resolution service provides advice on the use of arbitration and adjudication.

ARBITRATION

These proceedings are governed by the provisions of the Arbitration Act 1996 and the resulting awards are legally enforceable. If the parties involved wish to request this method of resolving disputes, they need to ensure that the provisions are written into their original agreement. In the RIBA standard forms of agreement the articles require the parties to select either arbitration or litigation as the final method of dispute resolution.

Frequently, the President of the RIBA is specified in the contract as the person to appoint the arbitrator. There is a President's list of arbitrators, which comprises professionals who have been recommended to fulfil this role. They will have sufficient legal understanding and practical expertise to deal with the types of dispute about which the appointment has been made. This list comprises architects, engineers and quantity surveyors, some of which are additionally qualified as solicitors or barristers.

LITIGATION

Disputes can, of course, ultimately be settled by using the formal legal process and taking the matter to the courts. Taking legal action is a serious, and potentially expensive step to take, so should not be undertaken lightly. If the sum of money you wish to recover through legal action is less than £5,000 your claim can be pursued in the Small Claims Court. Litigation in the High Court can be extremely expensive. Using the services of the Small Claims Court is intended to be as inexpensive as possible. However, whenever legal action is taken you must be prepared to risk losing, in which case costs could be awarded against you.

Small Claims Court:
www.moneyclaim.gov.uk

SUMMARY

- Good organisation is the key to effective credit control.
- The credit control process needs to be performed regularly and in a consistent way.
- New clients should be credit checked before any work begins, not only to see if they pay but also to see how rapidly and regularly they pay.

- Most payment problems stem from a misunderstanding between the architect and client about what was supposed to be delivered for the fee. The more precise the terms of any agreement can be the fewer payment disputes will arise.
- There is a statutory right to charge interest in the event of late payment and most agreements will include some provision for an interest charge to be made.
- Non-payment can often be the result of an invoice simply becoming stuck in the client's payment system. The credit controller's job is often like that of a plumber, unblocking the payment channels so that the funds can flow.
- Bad debts have a dramatic effect on profits as they drop through to the bottom line. Although the unpaid invoice may only represent 1 per cent of the practice's turnover non-payment may reduce the profits by 10 per cent or more.
- There are a number of formal procedures that can be used when all else fails ranging from mediation to full-scale litigation. The RIBA offers a number of services in this area and can support architects in these situations.

09 REPORTING

BRINGING IT ALL TOGETHER – REPORTING AT PRACTICE LEVEL

It is a key task of management to be able to gather and then successfully interpret all of the information that it has available to it. Over the years at SEH, I have continuously produced a monthly management pack of information that is easy and quick to update and - more importantly - is easy to digest. We believe that this pack now allows us to spot problems and react to them rapidly before they develop or become too threatening. The fact that we were able to survive the financial downturn of the late 2000s is at least some prima facie evidence that our approach was successful.

The process of successful financial management is somewhat like driving a car. You need to have the majority of your attention focused on the road ahead and what the other traffic (your clients and competitors) is doing. But you also need to be constantly glancing down at the dashboard to check that there are no warning lights flashing. When a light does show, you need to understand how serious the problem is - can you keep going for another few months and fix it later, or is it an urgent problem that could bring the whole practice to a sudden stop if not dealt with soon?

The previous chapters have looked at the various management tools and reports that you can use to get an idea of future fees and expenses.

From these you can produce a cash flow forecast that shows whether the financial future is likely to be a comfortable or bumpy ride.

The journey your practice is planning to take is mapped out by the annual budget. Progress is monitored on a monthly basis by comparing where you are with where you planned to be at this time. This is the satellite navigation system with which you can get back on track from wherever the practice finds itself.

The view through the windscreen of the road ahead is the captive fees forecast. As discussed in Chapter 6, that chart tends to have a familiar pattern, showing what the practice will be doing for the next month and probably for a month or two after that. The following three months after that are sketched in but the timing is subject to change. Beyond that period there may be captive fees of about 50 per cent of what may be needed, and then after that very little at all that is firmly committed. Most practices will have a forward order book profile that looks like this.

At SEH our 'cliff edge' tends to be six to nine months away. The trick is to ensure that it always remains that far away. If it does start to recede towards the left-hand side of the chart and become only three or four months away, then we know that we need to get busy trying to convert some of those 'possibles' to become 'captives'. Larger practices may well have a 'cliff edge' that is 18 to 24 months away, whereas a small practice may only have 3 or 4 months of confirmed work in front of them at any given time.

TURNOVER ANALYSIS

As well as ensuring that the practice is growing and making a profit, you need to maintain the balance of the expenditure profile or relative shape of the practice. The turnover analysis chart shown below illustrates this.

Turnover analysis
This chart analyses the turnover of the practice each year in terms of the percentage of the overall amount that is spent in each of the main practice areas.

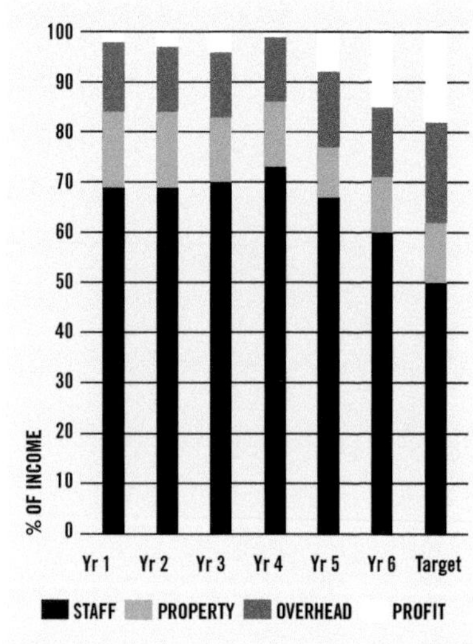

The turnover analysis chart uses the same categories of costs that are used for preparing the monthly flash report shown in Chapter 2 (i.e. staff, premises and all other overheads). The column on the right-hand side of the chart shows the target benchmark performance. In this example the target profile for turnover is:

- Staff – 50 per cent
- Property – 12 per cent
- Overheads – 20 per cent.

This leaves 18 per cent as profit or funds available to contribute to future growth and the development of the practice, as shown as the top slice of the bar. This represents an aspirational performance and in truth very few architectural practices are able to achieve a profit margin anywhere close to 18 per cent. In fact, many practices operate on a wafer-thin profit margin of 5 per cent or less. This is a dangerous way to operate, because it only takes a few things to go wrong for the practice to find itself in serious difficulty, as it will not have built up the financial reserves required to ride out any crisis.

Plotting the actual performance year by year against the benchmark in the same format enables you to see very quickly if the practice is moving towards the benchmark or, if not, to identify the area of expense that seems to be 'out of shape'.

In the example above, the practice made only a very small percentage of profit of 2 per cent in the first year. The problem is immediately apparent: far more was being spent on staff costs as a percentage than the target. Actually, the cost performance for the property and overhead categories was better than the target, but it was not enough to rescue the overall position.

Some small degree of progress is made in the right direction in years two and three but this is achieved by the further squeezing of property and overhead cost, rather than by addressing the real issue which is the proportion of total spend that is going on staff.

The situation reaches crisis point in year four. The property and other overheads are again kept well under control, but staff cost percentage increases once more and as a result almost no profit is made at all. At this level of profitability there will not be enough spare funds being generated to provide the money that will be needed to replace or upgrade computer equipment and other assets.

In the example, the crisis seems to have finally prompted the management of the practice to take some remedial action: in year five staff costs are finally reduced and a degree of profitability is restored. Further significant progress is made in year six and the practice turns in a very creditable 15 per cent profit.

It is very important to understand that these are *percentages* and are not absolute financial values. It is quite possible that the practice described above was enjoying rapid expansion in the years of very low profit margins. Almost all businesses find it hard to maintain their profit performance in terms of profit margin during a period of growth or contraction.

It's easy to see how this could happen in an expanding architectural practice. It is only natural when a practice wins a large new project that one of their first actions will be the recruitment of some new staff to help deliver the work. It is unlikely that the practice would have people ready and available just in case a new project was to arrive. Most practices tend to run a bit light on staff resources, because there always seems to be just a bit more work on hand than was expected. So sometimes there can be something of a panic reaction, especially if this is a new client and the practice is understandably keen to impress. That's fine while the new project is in its early design stages and is in a labour-intensive phase. Yet this time will pass, and people will gradually be released from the project onto other work. They may well have useful fee-earning work to do, but it may not be as profitable as the initial work on a major project. As discussed earlier in this book, fees tend to be front-loaded and the majority of the profitability on a project accrues in the early stages. In this way, additional resource costs get accidentally built into the practice, and the cost shape of the practice begins to suffer.

If nothing is changed, the cycle will repeat itself when another new project is won. Once again, after six months the practice has built in even more staff costs. This may seem to be acceptable as the practice is increasing turnover. It is only when the overall cost structure is reviewed in percentage terms, as shown in the example above, that the problem is discovered.

It is a common experience for a growing business to find that, despite a doubling of turnover, the amount of profit they have made in money terms has stayed the same or even fallen. This can be a source of great disappointment, prompting questions such as 'Why did we bother to do all of this extra work, if we are only going to end up with the same amount of profit as we had two years ago?'

The answer, of course, is to find a way to maintain the turnover at its new increased level, but to address the cost profile issues so that a satisfactory margin of profit is made. At an increased level of turnover, if the practice can successfully reshape its resources cost profile, then it should be well placed to make a healthy profit, which will provide it with choices and opportunities.

BENCHMARKING

While reviewing the performance of the practice at the overall level, it interesting and informative to see how the practices of comparable size are performing. Participating in inter-firm comparison exercises is a great way to do this and the RIBA now has its own service in this area.

The survey covers all areas of practice and although financial performance is covered extensively, there are also sections on marketing, the winning of work, the use of technology and human resource issues.

SUMMARY

› It is essential to learn how to read the signals indicated in the various reports and indicators, and avoid getting bogged down in any one particular area.

› Remember: successful financial management is like driving a car: most of your attention is focused on the road ahead (confirmed future fees income) while continuously glancing down at the fuel gauge (potential fees income), the oil pressure gauge (the cash flow forecast) and the engine warning light (the resources forecast) and also by looking in the rear-view mirror regularly and comparing the current performance to the budget and your performance in previous years.

› Keep an eye on the overall expenses profile of the practice (using the turnover analysis chart), especially in periods of rapid growth or decline.

› To avoid accidental build-up of staff numbers when you win new work, consider other forms of short-term resourcing, sometimes utilising temporary or contract staff or perhaps some form of outsourcing.

› It can be useful to participate in inter-firm comparison or benchmarking exercises such as the service offered by RIBA. This covers all areas of practice and peer comparison which can be very revealing.

EXIT STRATEGIES

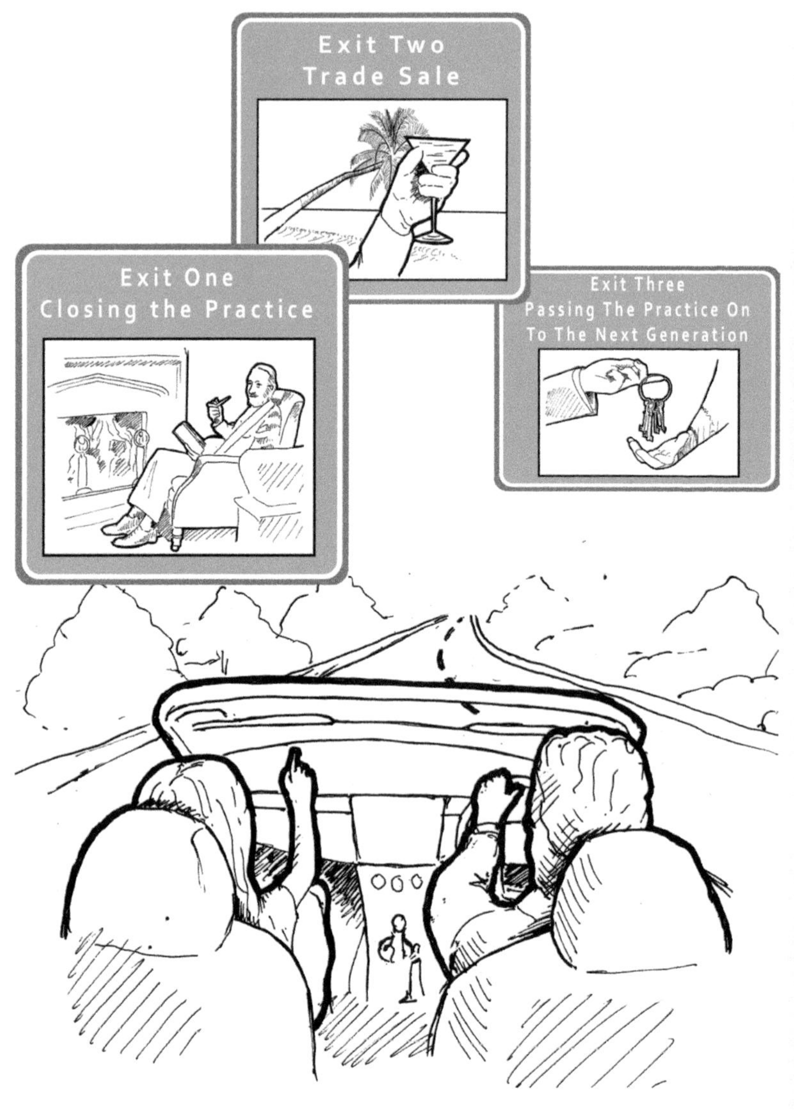

10

EXIT STRATEGIES

LEAVING THE PRACTICE – EXIT STRATEGIES

It may seem strange, but the best time to consider what you want to happen when you decide to leave the practice is at the very beginning when you are just setting up. Professional investors will always have an eye to their exit strategy from the outset before they invest their money in a business.

Chapter 1 discussed the way that you choose to operate, and the choice of business form (i.e. self-employment, partnership, limited liability partnership (LLP) or a limited company) and highlighted that this decision has a variety of far-reaching consequences. One of the most important of these is the way in which it determines the method that can be used to make an orderly exit from the practice.

In reality, of course, few people are that far-sighted, and the last thing on most architects' minds when they start out in practice is how they are going to leave. Indeed, most only give any thought to the subject at all when the inevitability of retirement or moving on is only a few years away. In general, architects are not good at early succession planning, and many practices fail to survive once the original founders have retired.

So this is an area which rewards careful advanced planning. Given a number of years, you can mould the practice into the optimum shape for a suitable exit. Ideally, you will be able to identify successors from within the business or, if that is not possible, have the time to identify the sort of people that would need to be brought in from the outside.

Bringing in a new person at a senior level is a particularly delicate process in a people-centred business such as architecture and requires careful consultation and communication. It would be wise to invest in the services of a specialist recruitment consultant or head-hunter, despite their fees, in order to ensure that this is handled professionally and does not destabilise the rest of the staff.

With careful planning it should be possible to exit at a time of your own choosing. Ideally this will be when the business is doing well and market conditions are relatively benign.

The consideration of exit strategy and succession planning should certainly be an agenda item for the five-year planning meeting, so that the practice can be gradually steered in the right direction.

WHAT ARE YOU LOOKING FOR WHEN YOU LEAVE?

Most architects are simply passionate about the architecture that they do and the impact that their work has on the lives of other people. They believe that their architectural vision and its inherent values are worth preserving and protecting by being passed on to a future generation.

However, most would also like to realise some financial reward for the work they have put in to the practice. Value will have been added over the course of many years of work, and it seems only fair that this value is in some way paid back to those who created it. From an accounting perspective, this value is reflected in the Balance Sheet of the practice when all of the assets and liabilities of the business are quantified for the year-end accounts. But this is a static view of the business frozen at a moment in time, and business valuations are more concerned with the practice's ongoing ability to generate profits.

There are three main options when it comes to realising a suitable reward for your labours: closing the practice; selling the practice; or passing it on to the next generation.

CLOSING THE PRACTICE

You could simply decide to select a date from which to cease practising. The outstanding amounts due on invoices from clients are then collected and any supplier's bills and other liabilities paid. The physical assets such as property, furniture or computer equipment can be sold for the best possible price. When all the outstanding financial transactions have been dealt with, including of course the final tax liabilities, the money remaining in the business can be paid out to the owners or partners. Depending on the residual value of this final distribution, this will be treated either as subject to income tax or capital gains tax. It is wise to consult with your accountant to make sure that you understand the tax implications of the timing of the closure of the business and the method used to take out any money that is left in the bank account.

TRADE SALE

A trade sale occurs when the business is sold to an outside party. This can be a good way to extract value from the business, but does of course require the practice to be in a form that would be attractive to a potential buyer. The main value of the business may be in the experience and contacts of a few key individuals and their loyal client following. Any buyer will be very concerned to know how feasible it would be to maintain the level of fees and profits that have been achieved in recent years, when those key individuals are no longer with the practice.

A common way of valuing a business is to apply a multiple of its average sustainable earnings over the most recent three or four years. The crucial word here is *sustainable*. The potential buyer may well require some form of 'earn out' period in which the former owners or directors stay in place for a number of years, until an agreed level of profit has been generated sufficient to justify the buyer's initial investment.

A prospective buyer is likely to employ their own accountants to undertake a 'due diligence' exercise. This is not only intended to check the accuracy of the figures that have been reported in the published financial accounts, but more importantly to take a view on the likelihood of achieving the forward forecasts that have been made for sales income and profits in the next few years.

These are the sorts of positive factors that would make a practice an attractive proposition to a potential buyer:

- Increasing and steady profitability on an annual basis
- Evidence of a high quality of service delivery, ideally with formal accreditation
- A history of innovative design with peer recognition
- Loyal clients who generate consistent repeat business
- A long-serving and committed design team
- Well-maintained premises and physical assets
- A good financial compliance record (i.e. the timely filing of financial accounts and tax returns).

PASSING THE PRACTICE ON TO THE NEXT GENERATION

A common exit method is to find a way to 'sell' the practice onto the next generation of management and this is where the choice of business form becomes an important issue.

PARTNERSHIP OR LLP

For a partnership or LLP this is often a straightforward process and is usually documented in the terms of the partnership agreement that was signed at the outset. The traditional model is for a new partner to buy in to the practice by subscribing an agreed amount of money as a capital contribution that remains in the business until their departure. This is often interest-bearing to give the partner some return on their money. For well-established practices their bank may offer partnership loan schemes, which are underwritten by the practice, to finance this commitment. While they remain a partner, they receive a portion of the profits made each year. In this way, the value they have contributed to the practice is paid out to them as it arises. Thus there is no need to debate this further on departure. When they leave, their original capital sum is repaid, together with any balance remaining on their current account (the amount of any as-yet-undrawn profits). An 'incoming replacement partner' then subscribes their initial capital and the overall capital funding level of the practice is maintained.

This model operates on a broad 'swings and roundabouts' basis. No account is taken of the consequences of unanticipated events that may have affected the partner, but which took place outside the period of partnership. For example, the firm may receive a refund from a supplier who discovers that an accidental double payment had been received in an earlier year. Strictly, this should be divided between those who were the partners at that time, but this would be too complicated to administer. Instead, the partnership will rely on the working assumption that these sorts of events tend to balance themselves out over a period of time.

LIMITED COMPANY

As noted in Chapter 1, the limited company format is more formal and legally structured. The ownership of the company rests with the shareholders. These shareholders may well also be the key directors of the practice, but there is an important distinction between these two roles. Anomalies can sometimes arise when a senior director who is an important member of the management team has a relatively small shareholding. When it comes to the exit process, what matters is the proportion of the business owned (as represented by the shares that are owned), not the importance of the individual to the management of the practice.

It is best practice to have a shareholders' agreement in place from the outset. This is similar to the partnership agreement described above, which documents how shares – and hence the underlying ownership of the business --are to change hands. Advice from a solicitor who specialises in this subject is essential, because this can be a complex and difficult area.

The process is somewhat similar to the writing of a will. Although the primary intention may be easily stated (e.g. on retirement shares will be sold for an agreed value to the other remaining directors) there is also a need to consider other possible scenarios:

› What happens if a shareholder or director dies unexpectedly?
› What happens if a shareholder or director becomes too unwell to work?
› What happens if the shareholder or director leaves to join a key competitor?

Even if none of the above applies and the situation is a straightforward onc of sclling shares on to the next generation, there is the vexed issue of determining the price at which this transaction should take place.

There are many ways to value a business, and this constitutes a whole subject in itself on which many books have been written. There is no single standard method of business valuation, because so much depends on the circumstances of the individual practice. Accountants and solicitors earn substantial fees from advising clients who find themselves without a valid shareholders' agreement in place, on the possible ways to arrive at a fair value for their shares.

This can become particularly difficult because each person in the negotiation will have different opinions on what the shares are worth. The shareholders' agreement is designed to deal with all of these potentially conflicting factors, including the method to be used for share valuation. In an ongoing business a multiple of recent sustainable post-tax profits is often used, but there are many ways that this calculation can be performed. The key is to reach an agreed method, to document it, and to insist that new shareholders sign up to its terms before they acquire any shares.

In recent years the government has been keen to encourage share ownership by employees and there are a number of schemes available designed to facilitate this. The schemes tend to change quite frequently, often following the Chancellor's budget, so it is wise to check with an accountant as to what schemes are currently available and how tax-efficient or appropriate they would be for your particular practice. At the time of writing the government has maintained the generous tax rates available under the Entrepreneur's Relief Scheme. Under this arrangement those who have been working directors in the business, and who own more than 5 per cent of the shares, can pay an effective capital gains tax rate of 10 per cent as compared to the standard rates of 18 or 28 per cent.

The LLP structure is often simpler and more flexible than the limited company and for this reason may be better suited to the majority of architectural practices, especially those consisting of ten people or fewer.

Leaving the practice is likely to be an emotional time, especially for the architect who has devoted most of their working life to building it up. This challenging period of transition can be made easier if the mechanics of the exit process have been thought through, agreed and documented well in advance.

SUMMARY

- The best time to plan an exit strategy is when you set up or join the practice in the first place, although this will be the last thing on your mind at the time.
- Most architects will be concerned that all of the work and effort which they have put into developing the practice is continued after they depart. However, they would also like to receive some financial reward for all of their hard work over the years.
- The practice itself, or its trading assets, can be sold as a whole to another firm or third party.
- The choice of business form (i.e. LLP or limited company), will affect the mechanics of selling the practice or passing it on to the next generation.

- It is important to take tax advice at an early stage of the process. For limited company shareholders it should be possible for the exit proceeds to be taxed under the more favourable capital gains tax rules.
- Leaving the practice is likely to be an emotional event. It can be made a little easier if the exit mechanics have been worked out well in advance. It would be a great shame if the final act in a long and creative career were to be a dispute over money with your former colleagues.

11

CONCLUSION

CONCLUSION

The consistent message running through this book is how important it is to continuously manage the working capital - and especially the cash flow - which is the lifeblood of the practice. The majority of construction projects are long term in nature and can take many years to reach handover and completion. Such projects are complex and involve many different people and organisations with conflicting agendas. It is unsurprising that the vast majority of projects end up being delayed. All of the different potential reasons for delay have an identical financial effect on the architect, which is that the payment of fees is delayed too.

It is always instructive to learn from the experience of others, so in this concluding chapter I have brought together some of the most common factors contributing to the failure of architectural practices. If you are following the advice in the earlier chapters you should already be well on the way to avoiding these problems.

However, no practice is working in an economic vacuum, and the financial uncertainty of recent years has taken its toll. So this chapter also includes an assessment of the economic problems we have all felt, what might lie ahead, and some crucial advice for all practices, whether they are brand new or long established.

WHAT CAN POSSIBLY GO WRONG?

FAILURE TO USE STANDARD AGREEMENTS

The great advantage of using standard RIBA agreements of appointment is that they automatically take care of the major areas of risk. They have been developed as a result of the practical experience and consequent feedback of many architects over many years.

However, clients will sometimes have their own form of contract for architectural services that they will insist on using. The reason that the client wishes to use their own contract is, of course, because they have had it drafted in a way that they consider to be favourable to them. It would be wise to consider the terms of such a contract carefully, taking particular note of where it differs from the relevant RIBA standard agreement.

The fees to engage the services of a good contract lawyer to review the client's contract will be money well spent and could prevent a major problem from developing later. The contract should also be forwarded to your PII provider for their review and comment before it is finalised.

FAILING TO INVOICE FOR WORK ON A REGULAR BASIS

The construction industry is used to the concept of payment becoming due when there is the completion of a particular stage or phase of the project. This is a reasonable approach, because the speed with which a piece of work is completed lies largely in the hands of the contractor. Most contractors are large businesses with financial resources to cope with these payment delays. But applying the same principle to the design team is very harsh. The timing of the receipt of their fees is now largely out of their control, and they tend to be much smaller businesses with much more limited financial resources.

Consequently, it makes sense to build in to the initial agreement the provision for the regular invoicing of fees, preferably on a monthly basis. As the previous chapters have shown, your major costs accrue on a monthly basis, so it makes sense to try to ensure that income is received at a similar rate. By agreeing to a staged payment fee schedule, you are reducing the risk of a six- or nine-month delay in receiving payment for your work. There is a considerable cost involved in the financing of this sort of payment delay.

FAILING TO COLLECT THE AMOUNTS THAT ARE DUE

The mechanics of credit control are discussed in Chapter 8. However, it is worth repeating the basic message, which is to ensure that all the money you are owed is collected promptly. Failure to collect fees can be caused by various delays and oversights. As a rule of thumb:

› First: check whether all the invoices raised and recorded by the accounts department were actually sent out to the client. It is surprisingly common to find invoices lurking in a pile of 'when I get around to it' paperwork on the project architect's desk, perhaps waiting for a covering letter to be written.

› Second: make sure there is a reliable system that alerts you when an invoice has passed its due for payment date. One person should be assigned the responsibility for tracking and chasing these outstanding invoices, and letting the relevant architect know if a problem has been encountered which will need their help to resolve.

- Third: deploy tenacity to pursue the debt until it is fully collected. The 'multiplier effect' means that even relatively small amounts can have a significant impact on profitability. It may be tempting to write off the final 'trivial' £2,000 that remains unpaid from a £100,000 invoice, but doing this will mean that the practice has to generate a further ten times that amount in fees to earn the profit to replace what has been lost by the uncollected amount.

NOT ASKING FOR ADDITIONAL FEES WHEN THE BRIEF IS CHANGED

I have noticed that many architects are not motivated primarily by financial reward. Indeed, it seems that architects could be the most generous of the professions, as they often seem to find themselves working for no fee at all.

Chapter 4 discussed ways to track the financial performance of an individual project. If the actual cost line is above the planned cost line, you are spending too much time on the project. This may be the result of inefficient working methods or faulty resource allocation, in which case it represents a genuine loss. More often, however, it is the result of the team trying to respond to a client's request for something extra or different.

We are all correctly advised to be client-led in our work and to be concerned to keep clients happy by answering their questions and responding positively to their demands. However, it is crucial to remain sufficiently alert to notice if you are being asked to do work that falls outside the scope of the contract. This is potentially good news for the practice, if the client is prepared to pay for this extra work to be done. If the client does not wish to pay, you should not be doing the work for free.

This does require an element of judgement and has to be conducted within the overall context of the client relationship management process. It is important to maintain good working relationships and to show that you can be flexible, but you simply cannot afford to give away 'the shop' too often. Clients and contractors will be skilled and experienced negotiators and will of course try to gain any financial advantage that they can for themselves. You must be smart enough to ensure that the practice is not being too generous. In general, you will find that the work will be valued and respected as a result.

NOT ASKING FOR ADDITIONAL FEES WHEN EXTRA WORK IS ADDED

This is a similar situation to the change of scope scenario described above. Yet this can be a more subtle variation that is harder to spot. When the brief changes everyone in the design team needs to be involved and the project will be noticeably different from the original plan.

What I mean here is that the basic design is not changed, but the client requests that some aspect of the design is revisited and alternative options explored. You may be interested in pursuing this design option too, so gladly embark on this piece of work without much thought for the time and cost implications involved.

It is crucial to develop a financial sensitivity to notice when work falls outside the scope of what you are being paid for and negotiate an additional fee accordingly.

At SEH we have become much better at spotting these sorts of opportunities over the years and we now routinely generate an additional 5–10 per cent of fee income just by paying attention to these opportunities as they arise. This is a good example of where investment in project management software can really pay off. By picking up cost overruns quickly, there will be a chance to identify and agree an extra fee before it is too late and the project has moved on.

FAILING TO MONITOR PROJECT COSTS AND CONTRIBUTION

You practice is more likely to be financially successful if you monitor the performance of individual projects and the work stages within those projects. Inter-firm comparisons such as those administered and published by the RIBA reveal that there is a correlation between those firms that make the most profits and those that monitor their project costs most closely.

We all know that some projects will not be as profitable as others. We may have chosen to accept a reduced fee in order to work with a new client, or to break into a new practice area. However, there is a danger that your practice might have a 'good reason' for every project not to make the required level of contribution, and hence end up being unprofitable overall.

LOW HIT RATE ON COMPETITIVE TENDERS

For most architects the initial winning of a project is the result of being successful in a competitive tendering process. This is particularly true for architects who do a lot of work in the public sector.

It is important to be realistic about the tendency of clients to commission architects to do more of the same type of work that they have done before. From the client's point of view the project represents a very substantial financial risk and we can understand their unwillingness to 'gamble' on an inexperienced architect. To their credit, some clients are prepared to give a new, young practice an opportunity to do the sort of project that they have never really done before. The client is hoping for the pay-off of a fresh and creative approach, but this is a risk that many are not prepared to take, especially in the public sector where accountability for the spending of public money is at stake.

While we would all prefer to design something new or work in a different sector, it is easy to fall into the trap of bidding for everything that you feel the practice could do or would like to do. Sadly, the result of this approach will usually be a lot of disappointment and rejection, and a lot of wasted time and money. Clients will tend to choose an architect with a proven track record or a recognised name.

The successful approach is to apply for work where you can offer some recent experience or unique advantage and firmly believe that this is a project that you should win.

At SEH, we have saved ourselves a lot of time, money and disappointment in recent years by being much more focused on our bidding process. Generally we try only to bid for projects that we feel 'has our name on it'. This helps to focus the marketing effort and improve the overall success rate.

These days public sector clients in particular are demanding an ever-increasing amount of supporting documentation to be prepared as part of the bid process. These bids are time-consuming and thus expensive to prepare, and it is important to ensure that the limited time available is used wisely. It can be easy to fall into the trap of being 'very busy' preparing bids and submissions. But if these are not well targeted, then the majority of the energy involved is being wasted, and this will ultimately be reflected in the reduced profitability of the practice.

POOR ESTIMATION AND FEE NEGOTIATION

Fees must be adequate to cover the cost of the job and to contribute to the overhead costs and profit requirements of the practice as a whole. This can only be done by taking the time to think through what will be involved in delivering the project and in particular the quantity and type of resources that will be needed, using a bottom-up analytical approach

You must be prepared to decide not to pursue a project if the fee is inadequate. There may be slack times when you might choose to do a piece of work at cost, just to generate the funds to continue to pay the salaries and other bills, but this should only ever be a short-term approach, because it will lead to severe financial difficulties quickly if applied on a regular basis.

FAILURE TO MANAGE THE DESIGN TEAM

Clients are increasingly looking for a 'one-stop shop' appointment of the design team. As the architect is the natural leader of the design team, it follows that they find themselves taking on this role more often than they used to, including managing various sub-consultant firms. There is often little or no reward for performing this additional co-ordination service. Indeed, it comes with its own considerable risks.

In practice, many sub-consultant firms are comfortable with a 'pay when paid' approach, although it should be appreciated that this is unlikely to be the correct contractual position. Standard agreements allow for the sub-consultant's payment terms to be longer than those of the architect so that the fees can be collected in advance, but this does not change the underlying legal position. When the architect has contracted with the quantity surveyor or engineer, it is the architect who is ultimately responsible for the payment of their fees.

It's very important to stay on top of the resources management process and to ensure that funds are flowing regularly from the client so that all members of the design team can be paid at the appropriate time.

HOW HAS THE FINANCIAL LANDSCAPE CHANGED IN ARCHITECTURE SINCE 2008?

The original version of this book was published just before the global financial crisis of 2008/9, which changed the financial landscape for us all. Although we all know that the construction industry is cyclical and that there will be ups and downs, nothing could have prepared us for the way the world changed so quickly in 2008.

Despite the frequent references I have made in this book about the long-term nature of the construction industry projects and the consequent effect that has on an architect's cash flow, this was different. The work position in our practice changed within a couple of days. A number of major projects, some at quite an advanced stage, were suddenly put on hold. Our captive fees income was suddenly reduced by 50 per cent.

Our resource planning charts soon started to tell us what we did not really want to know: that we would soon have too many people for the reduced level of work on the books. Our management systems allowed us to see this and react to it early, even though it did involve some very painful decisions on letting people go whom we really wanted to retain.

There is no doubt that in the difficult years of 2009 and 2010 there was intense downward pressure on fees. Other practices were fighting to survive just as we were, and consequently cut their fee proposals to the bone. We were astonished to see how low some competitive bids for work were. We could not see how any firm could possibly even cover their costs at the fee levels quoted.

Our clients knew that they were in a buyer's market and did their best to take advantage of the position. We managed our resource costs and cash flow very tightly and managed to come through.

The upturn came almost as quickly. In the Internet age sentiment as well as news travels globally very quickly. It seemed that suddenly we had all collectively decided that we had endured enough pain and it was all going to be alright after all. We have built our staff numbers back to their pre-2008 levels and as I write we are continuing to recruit and expand.

I have discussed the lasting effects of the last few years with a number of architect colleagues. They tell me that fee levels have largely recovered and that clients have learnt that you do tend to get what you pay for in architecture, as much as in any other area. Many clients had 'enjoyed' the low fee rates on offer in the difficult years, but discovered that their architects simply could not deliver the quality of work required at the fee levels they had agreed to.

Another effect has been that work is being commissioned in a much more piecemeal fashion, because clients are unwilling to commit themselves to more than the next stage of the work. Clients are also taking this opportunity to change their architects more frequently, and many projects will have been through the hands of a number of different practices before completion. Like most practices, we would prefer to be appointed to see the whole process through from design to completion, but that seems an increasingly rare situation.

ADDING VALUE

For a profession whose fees were already at the lower end of the scale compared with other professionals, the recession that began in 2008 was a disaster, and many firms, some quite high profile, did not survive. I believe this is partly because architects tend to have little or no financial reserves behind them to help them through the rough times. They do not have reserves because they have traded for too long on profit margins that were too slim and only allowed them to continue on a hand-to-mouth basis. It is possible that the next downturn is not too far away. The business cycle does seem to be accelerating as the world becomes more connected.

Throughout this book we have seen that the practice of architecture involves dealing with the problems that arise from long-term, complex construction projects. In that sense it is a profession that operates in a high-risk arena. Yet the traditional relationship between risk and reward somehow seems not to apply. Architects do not rank highly in the league table of professional pay scales.

I have often asked myself and my colleagues and students, why this is so. It's an interesting question to explore and one that always provokes heated comment and debate. I have not yet met an architectural student who does not hold strong views on this subject.

My personal view is that as a profession architects need to appreciate more fully the level of risk that they are asked to deal with on a daily basis. In general they manage this risk very successfully, and with this in mind architects should build their self-confidence and belief as a profession.

I believe architecture practices need to think much more in terms of the 'added value' of the work that is done. They should look for opportunities to work in partnership with the client, rather than just being another type of expense that the client seeks to minimise.

As information systems become increasingly automated and knowledge becomes more widely available, the professional adviser needs to reassess what it is that they can bring to the table. The client is looking for help to ensure that their project is realised on time and on budget. They want advisers to align themselves with their concerns and agenda. Architects need to retain their professional independence; but they also need to respond more readily to their client's entrepreneurial, environmental or social aspirations.

We should stand back sometimes and try to appreciate that the work we do affects people's daily lives in a profound way. I firmly believe that we should value the contribution that we make more, both in financial and social terms, and be bolder in asking to be rewarded appropriately.

GLOSSARY - DEFINITIONS

Profit & Loss Account - the annual statement of income and expenditure that shows whether a practice has made an overall gain on its trading performance. It will show the profit or loss that has been made before tax, the tax charge if any, and the subsequent profit after tax that is available for distribution to the owners or shareholders.

Balance Sheet - the statement of the total assets and liabilities of the business at a particular point in time usually the end of the financial year. Assets are divided into fixed assets such as property and equipment and current assets which includes cash in the bank, amounts owed to the practice by its customers and the value of work in progress. The balance sheet balances by showing the net asset position and who owns those assets. Usually this will be the partners or shareholders of the practice.

Cash flow forecast - a rolling statement of all of the cash inflows and outflows for the practice which predicts the month end cash balance for a number of months ahead. This is one of the most important reports for an architect to monitor in order to get a view of when a cash shortage problem may be approaching.

Input VAT - the tax paid to suppliers as a part of the settlement of their invoices.

Output VAT - the tax charged on collected to customers that is added to the practices invoices to clients.

VAT flat rate scheme (FRS) - a VAT simplification scheme offered by HMRC that makes the administration of the quarterly tax return easier and can result in a small gain for the practice.

USEFUL WEBSITES

ARCHITECTURAL PRACTICE

RIBA	www.architecture.com
RIBA bookshop	www.ribabookshops.com
Architects Registration Board	www.arb.org.uk
Architect's Journal	www.architectsjournal.co.uk
Building Design	www.building.co.uk
Fees Bureau	www.feesbureau.co.uk

CREDIT CONTROL

General advice	www.payontime.co.uk
Small Claims Court	www.moneyclaim.gov.uk
Insolvency service	www.insolvency.gov.uk

CONSTRUCTION PROJECT ACCOUNTING SOFTWARE

Union Square	www.unionsquaresoftware.com
Rapport	www.cubic-interactive.com

ONLINE ACCOUNTING SOFTWARE

Sage	www.sage.co.uk
Xero	www.xero.com
Freeagent	www.freeagent.com

PEER TO PEER LENDING

Funding Circle	www.fundingcircle.com
Rate Setter	www.ratesetter.com
Assetz Capital	www.assetzcapital.co.uk

CREDIT CHECKING

Dun & Bradstreet	www.dnb.co.uk

INDEX